60 IS THE NEW 100

GERARD KHO
JAMES SUNDRAM

notionpress
.com

INDIA · SINGAPORE · MALAYSIA

ISBN
Hardcase 979-8-89777-272-8
Paperback 979-8-89699-973-7

Contents

Contents

Part 03   TRINODIC LEADERSHIP MODEL: Decisive information system

Part 04   TRINODIC LEADERSHIP MODEL: A Future-centered strategy

Contents

Part 05   THE CULTURE GLUE

Acknowledgement

We, Gerard Kho and James Sundram, are deeply grateful to the many people who have been instrumental in bringing this book to life. As co-authors, we would like to share our heartfelt thanks to the individuals who have supported, guided, and inspired us along the way.

Gerard Kho

To my family, most importantly - Sansu, Clara and Oliver, Dad, Mum, Regina and Patricia. Your support and belief in me have been the foundation of this endeavour. Thank you for standing by me through every challenge and triumph.

To my mentors - Edmund Chan and Evelyn Biles. Your guidance has been invaluable in helping me grow as a leader and thinker. I am forever grateful for your support.

To my friends and colleague - far too many wonderful friends to list here. Your sharings, insights and encouragement have made this journey all the more meaningful. Thank you for your contributions!

➤ Acknowledgement ◄

James Sundram

To my family - My late Mother Sylvia Joseph, My wife Yew Jin, daughters; Juliette, Julienne and Jeselle. Your unwavering love and patience have given me purpose and the opportunity to be all I can be. My grandchildren Mason James, Aabel James and Lyla Mae, who have given me a new purpose and determination to strive. Thank you for encouraging me and giving me the space to pursue this vision.

To my friends and colleagues - Melvin and Gracia Goh Your support, encouragement and belief in the philosophies I pursue have enriched every aspect of this work. Thank you for believing in me and the support given during this journey.

Together, we also extend our gratitude to the leaders and organizations who shared their stories and experiences with us. Your openness and courage have deeply influenced the pages of this book.

Finally, and most importantly, we give all glory and honour to Almighty God. It is through His wisdom, grace, and infinite mercy that this book has been made possible. We take no credit for any of the inspiration or ideas within these pages, as they are a reflection of His divine purpose and guidance. He has been our ultimate source of strength, clarity, and purpose, and we are humbled to serve as vessels for His work. May this book glorify Him and inspire others to seek His guidance in all that they do.

➢ Acknowledgement ◄

To our readers: This book is for you. We hope it serves as a source of inspiration and guidance as you navigate your own leadership journey. Thank you for allowing us to share this vision with you.

With sincere appreciation,
– Gerard Kho & James Sundram

Foreword

Leadership, as we know it, is at a crossroads. The complexities of today's world demand more than traditional hierarchies or reactive strategies. It calls for a transformative approach—one that connects purpose, culture, and strategic foresight to create resilient organizations. 60 is the New 100: How Bold Leaders Shape the Future is not just a guide; it is an invitation to redefine the role of leadership in driving organizational success and shaping sustainable futures.

At the heart of this work lies the TriNodic Leadership Model (TLM), a groundbreaking framework that reshapes the way leaders think, act, and inspire. Rather than emphasizing agility or quick fixes, TLM focuses on three foundational pillars: inspirational leadership, decisive information systems, and future-centered strategy. These pillars address the core challenges facing leaders today—engaging people, managing knowledge, and positioning organizations to thrive in an uncertain future.

The authors begin by calling for leaders who inspire. Through the first pillar of TLM, they emphasize the critical role of purpose and mission in uniting employees and fostering a culture where individuals are motivated to go beyond transactional relationships. This form of leadership is not about dictating directives but about aligning people with a shared vision, creating the cohesion necessary for transformative growth.

The second pillar of TLM centers on building systems that efficiently gather and process information to enable informed decision-making. The authors argue that organizations must move beyond rigid hierarchies and empower individuals across all levels to contribute to decisions. By decentralizing information and encouraging collaboration, leaders create nimble structures that foster innovation and adaptability.

Finally, the third pillar—a future-centered strategy—compels leaders to look beyond the present and anticipate emerging trends. The authors introduce a forward-thinking approach that prioritizes foresight, strategic planning, and preparedness for a rapidly changing global landscape. This forward-looking mindset enables organizations to mitigate risks and seize opportunities that others might overlook.

What sets 60 is the New 100 apart is its deep understanding of cultural nuances. Drawing from Asia's dynamic context, the book weaves together insights on leadership, culture, and human behavior. It explores how factors such as collectivism, individualism, and organizational values shape the effectiveness of leadership practices. This makes the book particularly relevant for leaders operating in multicultural environments where the interplay of diverse perspectives is both a challenge and a strength.

More than a guide, this book is a call to action. It challenges leaders to rethink their roles—not as solitary figures but as stewards of knowledge, culture, and purpose. For those seeking to serve as advisors or partners in building transformative organizations, this book offers both the framework and inspiration to create meaningful impact. It highlights the value of collaboration and ownership in crafting sustainable solutions to the challenges of our times.

The TriNodic Leadership Model is a timely and necessary framework for leaders who aspire to leave a lasting legacy. Whether you are leading a corporation, guiding a team, or exploring opportunities to contribute as an advisor or stakeholder, this book equips you with the principles and strategies needed to navigate complexity, inspire people, and design organizations capable of thriving in the future. It is a must-read for those who believe in the power of leadership to shape a better world—and for those ready to take an active role in building it.

– Gerard Kho & James Sundram
Feb 2025

Part 01

REMODELLING LEADERS

Three-prong path into the future

When 60 is the New 100

The new world is one cruel, unforgiving place. Competition is of the cutthroat variety, with companies hungry for business pushing the limits to move into your comfort zone and steal your business. What can be done in situations like this?

Roll up your sleeves and enter the ring and fight it out? Give up and move into a new space? Or just blame the other party for being unfair and unethical?

Enter our TriNordic Leadership Model, which pushes for new thinking on what is needed to move and how to move. A central pillar of this approach is to move into a new management paradigm of acting quickly, even when you don't have 100 per cent of the information needed. In fact, 60 per cent is good enough to move.

Such thinking is especially important if you are leading organizations in the Asia region, where you are seeing the fastest growth rates this century. The numbers are staggering.

The GDP growth in some regions of Asia ranged between 313% in ASEAN countries to a staggering 575% in China in the space of only 12 years from 2001 to 2013.[1]

There is a downside to this stupendous growth, especially in countries that may not be resilient enough to weather an economic crisis. Many of the organizations in these countries were up and about only recently, and thus may not have experienced financial crises like those their predecessors went through. In the space of two decades, Asia two suffered economic meltdowns. The question is how many of the Asian firms that had been set up only in the last decade cope should there be another financial crisis. Are these ready for a crisis that could be just around the corner? Do they have robust structures to deal with such economic brutality? And how fast can they recover?

One word of caution, though. It is not just about the importance of having the capacity to withstand these economic pressures. It is also about how a company is able to maximize opportunities by being prepared structurally pre-crisis. This could ultimately give the company a head start and prepare it for the next cycle of growth in any post-economic downturn.

---

1   "ASEAN GDP and GDP per Capita," Asia Matters for America, accessed Nov 1, 2014, http://www.asiamattersforamerica.org/asean/data/gdppercapita

TLM Way to Human Capital Powerhouse

Now back to the TriNodic Leadership model that we mentioned at the start of the chapter. To ensure that a company is ready for the immense growth opportunities and possible challenges, leaders must first pay attention to the human talent that drives a company. There is no running away from it. Human capital is the powerhouse of any organization. Besides hiring the right talent, these people must be able to tap on each other to ensure that they are all in it for the same cause. This leads us to the need to understand not only why we must hire right, but also to create a workplace for these talents to grow, develop and excel.

We propose that leadership in Asia should look at three areas as proposed in the TriNodic Leadership Model (TLM). First, leaders have to be inspirational. In 2014, we did a survey on leaders aged of 35 and under in Asia. They were asked to list the quality of leaders they want as role models.[2] Inspirational leadership was that one quality that dominated. It ranked very high when another group of leaders above the age of 36 was asked to specify the quality younger leaders need to make their organizations fighting fit for the looming challenge.

Inspirational leadership takes many forms. Managers have to display a sense of mission and vision. They must be precise in their communication and honest with the difficulties the companies are likely to face. They have to inspire their employees and build resilience in their organization to take on the next challenge. They have to show what their plans are to gaining first mover advantage over the rest of its competitors. Not to forget the forging of a company culture and a value system which will then attract the right talent.

The company culture will include building a nimble team that will allow the company to manoeuvre easily to take advantage of changing environments. In order that the entire organization is able to move in unison, this culture must be one where it encourages employees to take calculated, informed risks. This first portion to the model starts in Chapter 2 describing how leaders must work with individuals within an organization to be united and ends in Chapter 4 by discussing how leaders have to inspire individuals in an organization in the Asian context amid the pressure of profit, profit and more profit (3P).

The second portion of TLM requires organizations to work on the organizational structure to ensure that it is able to gather

---

2   Kho. I., Survey Conducted on 1 Sep 2014 on leaders in Asia under the age of 35 and over the age of 36. Malaysia.

information as well as to make efficient decisions. To ensure that a company is able to gather the information constantly, and to have everyone in the organization receptive to new ideas, leaders must drive the whole organization to think about possibilities by encouraging the development of a variety of new ideas. Once these ideas are gathered and processed, decisions have to be made not only at the leadership level, but also right across the hierarchy of a company so that decisions can be made more efficiently in a decentralized manner. The organization can then reach decisions faster and in the process become more decisive. Time is of the essence as slow decision-making processes create disempowerment in the employees and they can become disengaged. Thus, for any company, the stumbling block is the existence of an inefficient decision-making process. The process can be made efficient when the organization is structured so that more people can make decisions. Decision making is not only the privilege or responsibility of the select few. As organizations expand in size and become more complicated, everyone within them must to be aligned with each other. The company must also have a system that encourages efficiency and effective decision making not only about things that matter today but also those related to opportunities that can give it a strategic advantage over its competitors. As highlighted in the survey conducted on the Asian leaders mentioned previously, one of the reasons leaders feel under-appreciated and frustrated is an indecisive organization. At the same time, one of the items which gives hope to the leadership of tomorrow is the ability and commitment of the leaders of the next generation to want to make decisions.

The third leg of TLM says that for all the above to happen, an organization must be future centered. It must incorporate strategic thinking right across the whole structure. Being strategic thinkers within an organizational context means that it has to introduce processes such as foresight to actively examine the drivers of change that could impact an organization. This requires learning perennially about the state of the current environment it is exposed to and to take those bits of information and then carve out relevant strategies. This process of continuous learning must form part of the culture of an organization for it to stand out from the rest. Having that capacity to continuously understand what the environment offers also makes the company and all its employees more future centered as opposed to only focusing on present-day issues.

The underlying assumption of the TriNodic Leadership Model is the need for the existence of an ideal company culture. The right culture will create that gel which accelerates and propels the growth of these organizations as they develop and expand. With the right culture, followers and leaders are encouraged to contribute and will be seen as a united team to grab the next big opportunity. This company culture will be covered in the final chapter of this book.

Don't Wait
to be Ready

In periods of economic prosperity, companies need to ensure that they are able to take advantage of the economic growth and seize growth opportunities to ride the wave. In these competitive global economies, many products and services are not only marketed locally but also into regional and global markets. Take Samsung. They started off as an electronics company manufacturing home appliances among other items. Samsung took advantage of the booming mobile phone market and evolved into one of the largest mobile makers overtaking traditional players such as Nokia and Siemens who were once giants and innovators in this sector. Apple has a similar story. They started with building the MacBook and Apple Macintosh personal computers. Today it has become one of the largest companies in the world and a large portion of their revenue comes from mobile devices such as the iPhone and iPad. They took advantage of the growing changing trend in technology and the speed of the Internet. Many companies have had such success stories as well. One question leaders have to ask is how one can start projects or initiatives to take advantage of new markets that could become the next big thing. The Internet was that one big thing. What is the next one? How can leaders identify an emerging trend and develop strategies to become the leader in a totally new emerging industry.

In the environment we are in, leaders must move and implement ideas before the full plan has been laid out. This would mean that we have to get the whole team to move before we are 100% ready. We must learn and adapt on the go, and to move when we are only 60% ready. In a fast-changing environment, what seemed like a 100% foolproof plan may not happen because the presumptions one had made at the planning stage could now have shifted because of the changing climate. Thus, it would mean that you may have to just start before you are ready and be flexible enough to alter the plan as you go along.

In an organization I was leading, one of the values we promoted was the value of urgency. How urgency was translated into action was that we were often called to act even when not all the evidence has been made available. When a colleague asks, "When do you want this to be implemented?", the answer was often, "Yesterday!". Our leaders often preached that "60 is the new 100". If you are 60% prepared, start work on it immediately and refine the plans as you move forward. Bishop& Hines (2006) says that organizations should understand the importance of making decisions without all the desired data as collecting more information could detrimental.[3]

Organizations today face challenges in environments where there are constantly many external changes.[4] To remain competitive, organizations need to undergo innovation and change processes to deal with these dramatic and constant changing environment.[5] Changes can come in the form of technology, products and services, strategies and issues revolving round the company's culture. Not to forget the dictum that staff are most valuable resource and they are the ones who implement the plans and strategies.[6] In the next few chapters, we have dedicated a section to helping leaders understand what it means to interact well with their employees and why it is important to do so and how this can be a strategy that needs to incorporate into the modern-day company.

3   Bishop, P, and Hines, A., *Thinking about the future: Guidelines for strategic foresight*. (Washington, DC: Social Technologies, 2006), LCC. ISBN: 978-0-978931-70-4, p.207.
4   Daft, R, *Organization theory and design* (Cincinnati: Southwestern, 2006): 411.
5   ibid, 412.
6   Gabrielsson, M., Seristö, H., & Darling, J. "Developing the global management team: a new paradigm of key leadership perspectives." *Team Performance Management*, 15(2009): 309.

Take Away Messages (Chapters 1-3)

- Understand the danger young companies in Asia could face if they are not structured to be prepared for crisis;
- Introduce the three parts of the TriNodic Leadership Model that would make staff think and engage across all functions within the company;
- Realize the TriNodic Leadership Model focuses on collective decision making and it creates an innovative culture that is constantly learning and processing information;
- Understand the need to be future centric to seize opportunities that are looming out there;
- Understand the ever-changing environment we operate in requires practising "60 is the new 100" philosophy.

TRINODIC LEADERSHIP MODEL

Leaders who inspire

Rebels with
a Pause

Organizations must start rethinking the type of people they want as leaders and workers. The belief that leaders must lead and followers must follow is becoming passe in a world that is chucking outmoded ideas and practices into the dustbin of history. Our firm belief is that organizations that want to be the leading lights must have rebellious people in thought and action. Not destructive rebels, but constructive ones. And these people, both leaders and workers, must know when to pause when they know that their ideas are not going to work. Humility is the watchword here. Learn to admit and move one.

Leaders must also be clear minded about the type of people they want. One constant is technology. In fact, every company needs it to drive its business. Leadership is something that is not taught and employees must watch their superiors and pick up the skills they know will be useful for their future. As Ms Teo Lay Lim, the former chairperson of Accenture Singapore said in an interview with BizBeat: "My leadership is to hire the best people and then empower them to do the job they you hired them for. It means trusting them, and definitely not micro-managing once they have earned that trust. It also means acknowledging that there is no one way to do things. A diverse team will come with different views, and collaboration will ensure that things get done with a holistic consideration of different perspectives."

The basic tenet of inspirational leadership is trust. And trust is a two-way road with both parties building a united organization that engages each other with clarity and humility. It is the starting point from where the TriNodic Leadership takes off.

Before we can achieve any significant change within any company, we need to understand how leaders and their employees work. We need to understand what drives leaders to behave the way they do, what inspires them to act the way they do and the different ways employees respond to leadership behavior. Once we understand the various types of employees, we can then focus our energy and make decisions on what initiatives or programs we can put in place to encourage them to engage with their leaders. Let us start by understanding the dynamics of each of these two groups.

Employees: Partners, Strong Implementers and Fence-Sitters

There are three kinds of employees and they are distinguished by two factors. The first is the degree of support employees give their leader. The second is at how willing employees are ready to challenge a leader's behavior and policies if these endanger the company's purpose or undermine its values.[7]

High Support

QUADRANT II IMPLEMENTER	QUADRANT I PARTNER
QUADRANT IV RESOURCE	QUADRANT III INDIVIDUALIST

Low Challenge   High Challenge

Low Support

Source: Chaleff, I. (2003). The courageous follower: Standing up to and for our leaders. San Francisco: Berrett-Koehler. (ISBN: 9781605092737)

---

7   Chaleff, I., *The courageous follower: Standing up to and for our leaders.* (San Francisco: Berrett-Koehler, 2003): 39.

Where employees offer leaders a high level of support, they can be great "partners" or strong "implementers" of the leader. Employees are ideal partners of a leader when they give vigorous support but at the same time will not hesitate to also question and challenge behavior or policies they are uncomfortable with.

In contrast employees who strong "implementers" are only interested in simply getting a job done and may not be inclined to challenge concerning issues they had already raise with their leader. It is unlikely they will correct a leader's value judgments under the circumstances.

There is another group that management gurus hardly mention. They are the fence sitters who don't have any strong feelings about which way the company is going. This group tends to be in the majority and can be the critical thinkers who help shift the ground, change mindsets of other groups to think about the company's prosperity and profitability.

Identifying the various aspirations of the different groups will allow leaders to determine the ability of their staff to influence the company in any process of change and transformation. Employees who can challenge when the need arises and model their behavior in a non-confrontational style helps establish integrity and earn everyone's respect.[8] What this all means for leaders is that there is a need to know how all the groups they are engaging. Understanding at which stage employees are, enables a leader to know how to further engage with them.

---

8   ibid, 51.

For example, having an employee who is an implementer may seem like a good thing but it doesn't necessarily mean that the person is engaged in making a decision. This type of employee or follower could simply be just order-takers and may not necessarily be good planners. They may not necessarily believe in the cause or the mission of the initiative taken by the organization. If followers are not engaged with their leader, the company chief needs to understand what he needs to do to improve this engagement process. This perhaps could involve including employees more often in the decision-making process. The ideal situation is to develop all employees toward being a true partner to the leader.

What Motivates Leaders

Now that we understand the way employees operate is dependent on their level of support for and extent of challenge on their leaders' mission, we need to understand why company chiefs operate the way they do and what inspires their behaviors. We can do this by understanding the motivation that drives their behaviors.

Journey of self-discovery

Leaders who constantly search for their purpose will ultimately make decisions that are more impactful and have an even lasting effect when these are better aligned with their values.[9] This focus on self-discovery is more likely to steer leaders away from the traditional motivations of money and hierarchy towards their empowerment and of others.[10] Knowing what

---

9   Graham, K. "Leading with purpose: a case for soul leadership." *Development and Learning in Organizations* 25 (2011): 5-7. doi: 10.1108/14777281111147026.

10   ibid, 7.

his purpose is will ultimately motivate a leader on how he should lead employees. Such a company chief will not focus only on developing quality leadership skills such as those related to vision, identity, influence, creativity, innovation and what would constitute making good decisions[11]. If this is the case, without self-examination, Graham (2011) says more often than not it leads to "only developing 'strong weaknesses' rather than enhancing unique talents". Leaders who embark on a self-examination exercise will be able to see issues objectively through different lenses. It will help them lead an organization on a correct path.

Trust and transparency

When external forces come into play, leaders must be able to sustain the trust and confidence of their followers. How they react to factors they can't control can influence perceptions, opinions and views of those they lead as well as stakeholders.[12] To keep their trust, there must be transparency in how information is gathered and decisions are made.[13] How a leader react to situations can also make a difference between real leadership and one that simply manages an employee's work.[14] These emotions are more sensitive when there are financial stresses or challenges where followers are more susceptible to fall into the trap of responding impulsively

---

11   ibid, 6.
12   Crompton, M. A. "The value of transparency. The Bottom Line." *Managing Library Finances*, 24 (2011): 125-128. doi:10.1108/08880451111169188, p.126.
13   ibid, 126.
14   ibid, 126.

to these issues without verifying what is true and what is not.[15] The transparency of a leader's communication, therefore, can establish the facts early on to avoid emotional uncertainty.[16]

When followers have not established a degree of trust with their leader, they are less likely to believe and accept his behavior and actions.[17] Transparency practised in the planning stages and a leader's actions are important in gaining the trust of followers, especially in times of negative events. The benefits are long term because they see their leader's confidence and optimism.[18]

Trust in a leader grows in social, cultural, institutional, and organizational and sub-organizational settings.[19] This is built upon on a daily basis and strengthens over time.[20] Moore (2011) states that trustworthy behavior is established when it contains a degree of "taken-for-grantedness". Where the motivation is trust, leaders tend to exercise a transformational leadership style. They are focused on encouraging employees to learn and exude creativity. This allows them to build trust with their followers.[21] A later chapter of this section will cover

---

15   ibid, 126.
16   ibid, 126.
17   ibid, 127.
18   ibid, 127
19   Moore, D. P., Moore, J. L., & Moore, J. W. "How women entrepreneurs lead and why they manage that way." *Gender in Management: An International Journal*, 26(2011): 220-233. doi: 10.1108/17542411111130981, p. 223.
20   Rhee, M. and Valdez, M.E., "Contextual factors surrounding reputation damage with potential implications for reputation repair." *Academy of Management Review*, Vol.34(2009) No.1, 146-68.
21   Brahnam, S.D., Margavio, T.M., Hignite, M.A., Barrier, T.B. and Chin, J.M., "A gender-based categorization for conflict resolution." *Journal of Management Development*, Vol.24(2005) 3: 197-208.

more on the qualities of transformational leadership and the impact they have on the leader-employee relationship.

A visionary drives job satisfaction

A leader's style is directly correlated with an employees' job satisfaction levels.[22] Research found employees to be more satisfied when their chief executives are visionaries.[23] Such a leader relies on followers who are committed to his vision and execute it.[24] He then can lead them effectively.[25] The visionary must therefore be in tune with his employees' needs.[26]

The motivation and empowerment of staff are predictors of their improved satisfaction.[27] In a visionary leadership, when the driving force is to improve staff satisfaction, the motivation of followers is crucial.[28] This comes in the form of decisions, job design and high expectations of performance and efforts, along with compensation and rewards when the followers'

22 Kantabutra, S., & Saratun, M. "Identifying vision realization factors at a Thai state enterprise." *Management Research Review*, 34(2011): 996-1017. doi: 10.1108/01409171111158965, p.1002.
23 Bass, B.M., *Leadership and Performance Beyond Expectations*, (New York: The Free Press, 1985).
24 Daft, *Organization*.
25 Avery, G.C., *Leadership for Sustainable Futures: Achieving Success in a Competitive World*, (Cheltenham: Edward Elgar, 2005).
26 Gilmore, T.N. and Shea, G.P., "Organisational learning and the leadership skill of time travel". *Journal of Management Development*, Vol.16(1997) No.4, 302-11.
27 Kantabutra, S. "Vision effects in Thai retail stores: practical implications". *International Journal of Retail & Distribution Management*, Vol.36(2008a) No.4, 323-42.
28 Awamleh, R. And Gardner, W. "Perceptions of leader charisma and effectiveness: the effects of vision content, delivery, and organizational performance". *Leadership Quarterly*, Vol.10(1999) No.3, 345-73.

actions are in line with a leader's vision.[29] Empowerment places emphasis on delegation and the passing of powers from higher organizational levels to lower ones.[30] Followers are given the ability to make decisions that are consistent with the vision of the leader. He empowers them to continue to act consistently in sustaining that commitment.[31] Where staff satisfaction is the key motivator to a leaders' behavior, he needs to lead by encouraging them to be involved in decision-making. A leader typically achieves this through coaching, informing and showing concern to his employees.[32] This leads to clarity of roles and a decrease in conflict, which are important factors that contribute to employee satisfaction.[33]

The learning tool

The learning culture of an organization is a social construct that is strongly influenced by a leader's actions.[34] He decides and implements changes that affect his followers' development. A leader's style influences the implementation

---

29 Maciariello, J.A., *Peter F Drucker on executive leadership and effectiveness*. In Hesselbein, F. and Goldsminth, M.(Eds). The Leader of the Future, (San Francisco: Jossey-Bass, 2006).

30 Carson, C.M. and King, J.E. Jr., "Leaving leadership: solving leadership problems through empowerment." *Management Decision*. Vol.43(2005): 1049-53.

31 Conger, J.A. and Kanungo, R.N., "Toward a behavioral theory of charismatic leadership in organisational settings." *Academy of Management Review*. Vo.12(1987): 637-47.

32 Dewettinck, K., & Ameijde, M. V., "Linking leadership empowerment behavior to employee attitudes and behavioral intentions: Testing the mediating role of psychological empowerment." *Personnel Review*, 40(2011), 284-305. doi: 10.1108/00483481111118621.

33 Steele, C. and Jones, C., *Networked Learning: Perspectives and Issues*, (London:Springer-Verlag, 2002).

34 Bass, *Performance*.

of changes in an organization and this dictates its learning culture.[35] A collective and inclusive style serves to inspire and motivate followers to participate in learning activities.[36] The transformational approach works by nurturing followers through inspiration where any changes implemented are conducted in an organized and purposeful manner.

> **Take Away Messages (Chapters 4-6)**
>
> - Individuals are able to understand what drives leaders to behave the way they do by examining the motivation behind their behaviors;
> - There are three types of followers and they are defined by the extent of their support and capacity to challenge leadership.

35 Garcia-Morales, V., Matias-Reche, F. and Hurtado-Torres, N. "Influence of transformational leadership on organisational innovation and performance depending on the level of organisational learning in the pharmaceutical sector", *Journal of Organisational Change Management*, Vol.21(2008) No.2, 188-212.

36 Bass, *Performance.*

Orbit Around
the Mission

In the previous chapter, we explored the three kinds of followers and discussed what motivates a leader's behavior. In this chapter, we will explore how a company can develop a united workforce by encouraging leaders to inspire employees through focusing on how they both can engage each other. Understanding the significance of this is important in any change initiative, whether it is to be future centric, decentralize or make better decisions across the hierarchy of an organization.

Bonded by Purpose

Leaders and employees are bonded through a common purpose. Let's begin by understanding the importance of this and how it results in a triad relationship that includes purpose, an atomic glue that binds the two together. A purpose gives a reason for a company to exist and meaning to the activities it partakes.[37] Conventional thinking is that employees orbit around the leader. What it should be is both employees and

---

37   Chaleff, *Follower*, 13.

leaders orbit around the purpose. But when purpose is neither clear nor motivates, they will only pursue their own and not the common interest. Therefore, for an effective company to operate, the leadership team and employees must first clarify their common purpose. Only then, can they be mobilized easily to steer through treacherous passages and take on new opportunities aggressively. Defining purpose is a critical act of strong leadership and courageous followership. When purpose and mission is clearly established, they can be clearly aligned and in sync with each other.

Leading to such an alignment both parties must first share common aspirations or value systems.[38] The mission, as Winston & Patterson (2006) states, is to "create an image in the minds of followers that they belong to something bigger and more important than just an individual job."[39] Once the purpose, mission and values are clarified, leaders and employees can interact and discuss perhaps even areas of discontentment so that everyone is able to move towards a preferred future that is commonly aligned. Such coming together will motivate all to act appropriately where employees are encouraged to play a larger role in leading change while the chief executive takes on the minor role.[40] This collaboration ultimately helps a company to adapt to internal strategic reshuffles or to the external forces that force change.[41]

---

38 Winston, B., & Patterson, K. "An integrative definition of leadership." *International Journal of Leadership Studies,* 1(2006): 12.
39 ibid, 12.
40 Kelley, R., *The power of followership.* (New York: Currency, 1992).
41 Winston & Patterson, *Leadership,* 28

Dynamic leaders are now fundamentally the spark and flame that ignite action. They generate and focus power, and employees are the guarantors of the beneficial use of this.[42] For any organization to succeed, it is therefore essential the mutual collaborative efforts between leaders and employees are aligned to ensure peak performance.

____

42 Chaleff, *Follower*, 13.

Make Room for Risks and Mistakes

To create an engaged group of individuals, it is not enough for employees to simply understand what drives leadership to behave the way they do. The alignment between both cannot be attained without leaders understanding they need to forgive the shortcomings of employees'. This will encourage both groups to forge a closer working relationship. The leader, of course, is entitled to expect high standards of performance from employees but must be in an environment where they are able to learn from mistakes.[43] When a leader is consistent and predictable in this area, followers are more willing to take risks as they can predict the outcome if they fail.[44] Therefore, instead of focusing on "blame and persecution", leaders would do well to identify the underlying causes of problems and find solutions to correct them.

---

43 Winston & Patterson, *Leadership*.
44 ibid, 31.

Once these solutions are found, leaders are effectively exercising "mercy" on their employees. They will be reassured that when they fail unintentionally, they have a leader who will support them and provide training to address the issues to encourage employees to continue to take calculated risks. Leaders are ultimately accountable to management on how they supervise employees. This is not to say that a leader must be forgiving in all circumstances. He must still exercise responsibility in reprimanding subordinates if their actions are inappropriate but with the aim of helping them avoid such mistakes with proper measures.[45]

Critical Thinking Produces Discernment

For leaders to handle any change, crisis or to get a buy-in from followers, it is important critical thinking forms the basis of convincing arguments for their positions. It will help a leader build up information through facts and communicate it wisely.[46] According to Winston & Patterson (2006), critical thinking typically requires, "the ability to build and discern inductive or deductive arguments, to determine if the data is qualitative or quantitative and how much reliance can be placed on any argument." Ultimately, the extent of leaders' capacity to drive any change using such skills leads will help them present persuasive arguments.[47] In the later part of the book, we will discuss how leaders can build an information bank through creating a culture that is focused

---

45 Miller, C., *The empowered leader*. (Nashville: Broadman and Holman,1995), 37.
46 Winston & Patterson, *Leadership*, 17.
47 Cederblom, J., & Paulsen, D. W., *Critical Reasoning (5th ed.)*, (Belont: Wadsworth, 1997).

on learning 24/7. This bank will help them craft solutions by engaging employees to arrive at wise decisions through an anticipatory futuring process of identifying and prioritizing the issues.

The Right Talent Are Partner Employees

An obvious area to ensure a leader is able to undertake any change initiative effectively is to exercise the stringent practice of identifying the right talents in the business.[48] Without such people in their ranks, it is difficult to implement change. This ultimately will affect a leader's reputation and he will face challenges to lead any initiative.[49] At the very least, a follower has to be seen to support, and be committed and loyal to a leader. This does not mean that an employee merely follows blindly, but must also be able to challenge his chief. Followers essentially are a team of counsellors for any leader and both parties support each other through proper communication, cooperation and collaboration.[50] Where their support and values align, it will lead to a good organizational fit.[51]

---

48 Collins, J., *Good to great: Why some companies make the leap….and others don't*, (New York: Harper Business, 2002).
49 Miller. *Empowered*, 39.
50 ibid, 39. 168.
51 Brown, D.E., Ledford, Jr., G.E., & Nathan, B.R. "Hiring for the organization, not the job." *Academy of Management Executive*, 5(1991): 35-51.

Transformational Leadership

An ideal leadership style is to build engagement and connection among employees, and influence them to innovate and improve how a company operates. This is achieved when everyone is provided with support that encourages creativity and tolerance of differences.[52] Such a leadership style is ideal for creating companies that strive to constantly adapt through the integration of their continuous learning mechanisms. If a company is able to constantly learn from its environment, it has taken the first step to becoming an outfit that adopts strategic thinking. More about this in subsequent chapters of the book. Essentially leaders can encourage individuals to be a learning-inclined group by providing them with positive feedback and to acknowledge and celebrate their contributions. This encourages employees

---

52 Elenkov, D. S., & Manev, I. M., "Senior expatriate leadership's effects on innovation and the role of cultural intelligence". *Journal of World Business*, 44(2009): 359.

to be identified with the team and it will improve the company's performance.[53]

Transformational leadership is the ideal style to build engagement between managers and employees, and the goal is to forge a bond among all. Bass and Avolio (1985) mentions that transformational leadership is constructed on four broadly defined behavioral scales. These illustrate how a motivation to build a culture of learning and leadership styles are interrelated. One of these scales focus on the impact that intellectual stimulation have on employees. A leader usually encourages followers to adopt critical thinking, the questioning of assumptions, and he often endorses new strategies and techniques they present to solve challenges. This stimulation in thinking encourages the search for new solutions to challenges through learning.[54]

In employing a transformational leadership style, a leader acts as mentor and guide employees through a learning journey that focuses on each employee's strengths and weaknesses by inspiring and developing them.[55] Mentoring also helps everyone to understand a leader's initiatives of change. However, as with any mentoring method, it should be mentoree centered,[56] and focused on that person's needs. A mentoree should ideally also draw up his own requirements of what

---

53 ibid, p.360.
54 Jogulu, U., "Leadership that promotes organizational learning: both sides of the coin." *Development and Learning in Organizations*, 25(2011): 11-14. doi: 10.1108/14777281111147044. p.12.
55 ibid, 12.
56 Perren, L., "The role of e-mentoring in entrepreneurial education and support: a meta-review of academic literature." *Education + Training*, 45(2003): 517-525. doi: 10.1108/00400910310508900.

he expects out of a leader's guidance. After all, if employees recognize their own aspirations in the leader's vision, they follow their own light, which the leader intensifies.[57] Promoting learning encourages the rank and file to also view their roles and responsibilities beyond their personal self-interest.[58] This learning culture will also ultimately increase an organization's capacity to adapt by being responsive and allocating the right resources in a rapidly changing external environment.[59]

The last few chapters of this book serve to explain the importance people play in determining if an organization is able to take on the changes. Indeed, discussing about how to lead individuals who are connected to one another becomes the starting point for any company that seeks to impress the market with its next big idea. We have shared extensively about why leaders behave the way they do. This can complement our understanding of how employees react to leaders. Ensuring that the two groups understand how each other operate allows us to discuss about how they can remain connected in any change initiatives.

In the bigger scheme of things, the two connected groups makes it easier to implement a streamlined decision making and knowledge management framework. This is essential as it not only ensures the organization remains relevant in fluid environments but allows it to reach a consensus quickly to take advantage of opportunities.

Before we move on to how an organization can become more decisive, we want to explore the challenge that most face, which

---

57   Chaleff, *Follower*, 13.
58   Jogulu. *Learning*.
59   ibid, 11.

is how individuals respond in an environment that is perennially preoccupied with making more and more profit. The obsession with profit is certainly a characteristic of growing economies in Asia. The good news is that a leader can still continue to inspire followers and reach a state where both are engaged, even in this profit obsessed environment. There is no conflict between these two agendas. Creating connectedness among everyone in a company and profit, profit and yet more profit.

Take Away Messages (Chapters 7-9)

- Individuals in an organization understand what it takes for leaders and employees to remain connected with one another;
- Appreciate the importance of leaders providing support and understanding to followers in this engagement process;
- Leaders understand the importance of providing the ideal environment for followers to make mistakes and contribute. This inspires and encourages them to grow within an organization;
- Leaders understand that the ideal leadership style in creating a connected team requires the introduction of one that is transformational.
- Individuals are able to understand what drives leaders to behave the way they do by examining the motivation behind their behaviors;
- There are three types of followers and they are defined by the extent of their support and capacity to challenge leadership.

The 3Ps in a Changing Asia

Profit, Profit, Profit or the 3Ps is the one thing that is creating a piling pressure on leaders today. This pressure point is there in the midst of all that is happening in Asia, with its changing economic and social landscape. A local business is now charged with expanding out into the region as it strives for more and more profit.

We hear it all too often that when management overachieves their target in one calendar year, they are given an even higher one in the next year. Let's push, push and push. Let's be the fastest growing company and take over the world. Asia is at a season where many live with the hope that everything and anything is possible especially when many economies in the region have experienced astronomical growth. They were in poverty just a few decades back but today the landscape in these cities is occupied by cranes as they build newer, taller and larger skyscrapers. New expressways are sprouting as growing cities establish connection with regional centers where most commercial activity takes place.

Leaders today are not only expected to steer companies through economic transformations but are called to do so under constant pressure for the capitalist maxim of profit and achievement. The 3Ps is the pressure in developing countries. In China the prevalent collectivist culture used to be characterized as "We", where the members of a society see themselves as part of a group[60].

This is opposed to the "Me" culture where they view themselves as isolated individual entities. However, Lu (1998) states that this individualism culture will increase with a corresponding rise in wealth, industrialization and economic reform.[61] Along with modernization, individualistic orientation is becoming more prevalent.[62] The collectivism culture, prevalent in such countries as China, may even be replaced by individualism through the process of modernization.

Many societies and organizations, especially in Asia, aggressively pursue excessive profits and in their zeal for growth, they glorify and reward excessively the achievements of individuals. Modern day global leaders must be aware of this increasing trend towards the "Me" culture. Economic systems and leadership models that thrive on individualism and reward rampant competition are unsustainable in the

---

60   Ryu, S., Eun-Ju, L., & Won, J. L., "A cross-cultural study of interfirm power structure and commitment: The effect of collectivism." *The Journal of Business & Industrial Marketing*, 26(2011): 92-103. doi:http://dx.doi.org/10.1108/08858621111112276. p.93.

61   Lu, X., "An interface between individualistic and collectivistic orientations in Chinese cultural values and social interactions." *The Harvard Journal of Communications*, 9(1998): 91-107. p.104

62   ibid, 104.

complex challenges modern economies face.[63] This chapter offers insights into the changing environment of Asian economies. This change may not be all bad if we know what is driving it. We need to understand what is happening. There is hope that despite these seemingly exuberant economic boom and sometimes chaos, there are areas a company can focus on and ensure that as long as the basics are monitored constantly, the 3Ps can continue to exist in any business objective. The ideal leadership style that offers hope for a solution to this dilemma will also be discussed. Leaders need to continue to inspire employees that they do have control over outcomes even under pressure from the 3Ps.

---

63   Piterman, H., "The Leadership Challenge : Rediscovering the Voice of Reason." *Organisational & Social Dynamics*, 10(2010), 199.

The We vs Me Relationship

Whether an environment is more "Me" or "We" dictates the balance of a relationship between individuals and collectivism prevailing within a society.[64]

The mutual benefit of 'We'

In Eastern cultures, "We" connotes concern for exchange partners and placing their interests on par with one's own.[65] It suggests the promotion of sharing. Individuals in a society possessing more "We" values can commit to a relationship with a partner with the emphasis on developing a harmonious relationship between different groups of people.

---

64 Papamarcos, S. D., Latshaw, C., & Watson, G. W., "Individualism-collectivism and incentive system design as predictive of productivity in a simulated cellular manufacturing environment." *International Journal of Cross Cultural Management*, 7(2007):253-265. Retrieved from http://0-search.proquest.com.library.regent.edu/docview/221216078?accountid=13479 p. 255.ryu

65 Ryu, Eun-Ju & Won, *Cross-cultural*, 93.

In high "We" dominant societies, the question is whether the parties involved are assigned equal priority for their own benefits with those of their exchange partners. The exchange side receives benefits when its partner promotes its interest and is likely to have an intention to continue their relationship. Therefore, "We" cultures contribute to a high level of commitment. In such societies, group members tend to perceive themselves as sharing a "common fate" that provides a basis for developing a long-term relationship with partners. There is a "We" consciousness that translates into emotional dependence of the individual on society, a felt need to belong, willing subordination to individuality and private life, and a belief that value standards differ for in- and out-group members.[66] This culture is one that ensures all parties benefit from the relationship, where no one side has taken advantage of the other. All look forward to a mutually beneficial relationship.

The self-interest of 'Me'

Societies of this nature tend to emphasize self-interest and the maximization of one party's benefits without a great deal of consideration for exchange partners' gains.[67] They tend to pay less attention to a relationship, are more task-oriented and define themselves as autonomous entities, independent of any group. Each side wishes to protect the benefits it derives from any relationship with the sole motivation of wanting to maintain good ties. This commitment is motivated by achieving their respective successes.

---

66   Papamarcos, Latshaw & Watson, *Individualism*, 256.
67   Ryu, Eun-Ju & Won, *Cross-cultural*, 94.

High "Me" cultures imply a preference for a loosely knit social framework within which people are supposed to take care of themselves and their immediate families.[68] "We" cultures, on the other hand, prefer a tightly knit social framework in which individuals are integrated emotionally into an extended family or other in-group who will protect them in exchange for unquestioned loyalty. This self-interest and "I" orientation result in an emotional independence, with an emphasis on initiative, achievement and rights, and a universalistic feeling that value standards should apply to all.

In "Me" cultures, self-interest is a driving force, overriding the importance of group harmony. Workers in such societies feel empowered to ask for what they, as individuals, would like.[69] In, contrast, group harmony and consensus are of utmost importance in "We" countries. Conflict is resolved via consensus and compromise, and hierarchy is not required to impose authority since loyalty is so well internalized.

---

68 Papamarcos, Latshaw & Watson, *Individualism*, 256.
69 Papamarcos, Latshaw & Watson, *Individualism*, 256.

Masculine and Feminine Cultures

A leader has to be aware of changes in the organization, especially when it is moving away from the traditional "We" culture and evolving to a more "Me" way of life. In addition to "Me" and "We", a masculine cultural dimension now adds to the complexity of what a leader has to be aware of before deciding which style to adopt to increase the effectiveness in steering an organization. In such environments, both performance and assertiveness orientation suggest the emphasis is on competition, achievement and individual outcomes.

They focus on results and are less concern about the means of achieving them.[70] This is consistent with societies that exhibit masculinity characteristics.

---

70 K, P. P., Bronson, J. W., & Cullen, J. B., "Does national culture affect willingness to justify ethically suspect behaviors? A focus on the GLOBE national culture scheme." *International Journal of Cross Cultural Management*, 5(2005):123-138. Retrieved from http://0-search.proquest.com.library.regent.edu/docview/221216486?accountid=13479. p.134.

This culture values competitiveness and assertiveness, whereas one that is feminine prizes people and relationships.[71] In masculine societies inhabitants are more ambitious and voracious for wealth and material possessions. Organizations tend to be more performance driven and pay less attention to building interpersonal relationships in the work place.

Prominent values are assertiveness, acquisition of money and material things and uncaring towards others. The masculine curiosity in accumulating wealth reflects an exchange of behaviors for extrinsic rewards.[72] Confidence, decisiveness, and ruthless individualism are rewarded in these business environments.[73] In addition, competitiveness, individualism and results-orientation breed a hero mentality.[74] And the focus is on growth, market dominance and expansion.

Performance oriented societies tend to value people who can perform and produce results.[75] They emphasize personal outcomes and value results, assertiveness, competition and materialism. Because achievement is priorities in masculine cultures, people are also more likely to accept behaviors generally considered unethical.

---

71 Skerlavaj, M., Su, C., & Huang, M. (). "The moderating effects of national culture on the development of organisational learning culture: A multilevel study across seven countries." *Journal for East European Management Studies*, 1 (2013): 97-134. Retrieved from http://0-search.proquest.com.library.regent.edu/docview/1321663409?accountid=13479. p.106.

72 Bashir, M., & Gazanfar, F., "The role of power distance and masculinity in the relationship between high performance work system and academic faculty job satisfaction in Universities of China." *International Conference on Management, Leadership & Governance* (2013): 444.

73 Piterman, *Leadership*, 192.

74 ibid, 191.

75 Bronson & Cullen, *Culture*, 126.

On the other hand, a feminine culture stresses openness in communications, participatory decision making and less hierarchical structures. Leadership style tends to be relational, holistic, process-oriented and transformational rather than transactional.[76] Feminine values are more concerned for people and their quality of life and works on the principle of interdependence. In masculine societies, feminine behaviors such as sensitivity and vulnerability are not well received.[77]

---

76   Orser, B. J., Elliott, C., & Leck, J., "Feminist attributes and entrepreneurial identity." *Gender in Management*, 26(2011), 561-589, doi:http://dx.doi.org/10.1108/17542411111183884. p.566.
77   Piterman, *Leadership*, 192.

Information and Relationships

As companies strive to become relevant and pay more attention to manage information that forms part of the decision-making process, leaders have to adapt. This adaptation depends on how cultures perceive knowledge sharing and what followers expect of their leaders. Examining the interplay of "We" societies and masculinity dimensions to understand how a culture functions provides a more realistic approach to leadership today. Me-We orientation is viewed as the major distinctive influence on how various groups of people process and deal with information.[78] In "Me", people perceive information to be independent of its context, while "We" stresses the context in which information is discerned, interpreted and shared.

Aggressive Cultures

To what degree masculinity negatively affects knowledge sharing among people in a company depends on the level

---

78 Skerlavaj, Su & Huang, *Natural Culture*, 105.

it is inherent in a society.[79] Cultures of low masculinity provided more support to collaboration and this leads to a greater level of research and development activity.[80] A high masculine inclination places a greater emphasis on individual achievement and competition over interpersonal collaboration and the forging of relationships. A masculine culture may be able to attain satisfactory performance and profits in the short term, but encounters greater challenges and difficulties in developing a culture that engages people which is important for sustainable growth.[81]

Sharing Information in We and Me Societies

The "We" inclined group leads to solidarity and frequent information exchanges among its members, This, in turn, leads to intensive knowledge sharing and facilitates not only this, but also motivates them to interpret the information.[82] In "Me" societies, people are less likely to engage in collective exchanges, clarify, understand or interpret acquired information based on organizational, social and cultural contexts.

Nations with stronger "Me" culture exhibit a weaker positive relationship from acquisition information and to interpretate it in a learning culture.[83]

In companies saturated with the "Me" mentality, managers have to cultivate a working environment that values peer-

---

79   ibid, 107.
80   ibid, 107
81   ibid, 124.
82   ibid, 105.
83   ibid, 105.

to-peer information sharing and knowledge transfer.[84] Procedures and rules should be established to prevent anyone from withholding information for their own interests, and encourage incentives to reward collective learning and sharing.

---

84 ibid, 125.

Impact of Cultures on Behavior

In "Me" cultures that exhibit aggressive characteristics, there is the willingness to justify ethically suspect behaviors.[85] In these societies, there is the emphasis on preserving harmony within a group, especially where ethically suspect behaviors present the risk of disturbing the construction of the collectivist societies.[86] In feminine or relationship-based cultures, there is less likelihood to justify ethically suspect behaviors. Since individualism and collectivism refer the extent to which identity is based on self, performance oriented societies can be assumed to be more individualistic in character.[87]

The process of converting interpreted information into actionable knowledge varies between "We" and "Me" cultures.[88] Intensive interpersonal relationships facilitate the transfer of tacit knowledge and "We" cultures are more likely to make

---

85 Bronson & Cullen, *Culture*, 134.
86 Bronson & Cullen, *Culture*, 134.
87 ibid, 126.
88 Skerlavaj, Su & Huang, *Natural Culture*, 106.

behavioral and cognitive changes based on social influences and collective values. In "Me", members tend to pay less attention to the shared context of information interpretation, and are less motivated and capable of converting knowledge into behavioral and cognitive changes. Members are therefore more likely to observe, share and practice values in the "We" than "Me" cultures.

"Me" Individuals Are Not All Bad

Tu, Lin & Chang (2011) acknowledge that cultures with high levels of "Me" elements result in more time spent conducting direct communication.[89] In "We", people are typically more concerned with group and social welfare. In these societies, more time is spent on indirect activities unrelated to communication. The concepts of "Me" and "We" to explain cultural distinctions have since been applied to the individual and are conceptualized as personality traits that can possibly adapt to situational demands.[90]

"Me" members have their personal goals and attitudes that take precedence over those of groups. Finkelstein (2012) suggests that though there is a divergence between individualists and collectivists, their willingness to help or volunteer in activities does not differ. The only difference are their motives. In light of this, a leader may have individualistic or "Me" employees

---

89   Tu, Y., Lin, S., & Chang, Y., "A cross-cultural comparison by Individualism/ Collectivism among Brazil, Russia, India and China." *International Business Research*, 4(2011):175-182. Retrieved from http://0-search.proquest. com.library.regent.edu/docview/863813074?accountid=13479. p.179.

90   Finkelstein, M.A., "Individualism/Collectivism and Organizational Citizenship Behavior: An Integrative Framework." *Social Behavior and Personality.* 40(2012): 1633-1644. p.1635.

serve a common goal in a company that operates in a more collectivistic or "We" environment. Leaders simply alert individuals to the benefits, opportunities and rewards specific activities that provide for any change.[91]

---

91 Finkelstein, *Individualism*, 1641.

Leadership in
3P Cultures

Though the definitions of cultures differ, they are recognized as important influences on the behaviors of everyone.[92] Individual motivation and leadership styles can be traced to differences in cultural orientation. An individual with "We" values is more apt to fostering collaboration, strengthening the team, enlisting others towards a shared vision, and celebrating team accomplishments.[93] A transformational leader in this sense is more inclined to lean towards a collectivist or "We" culture.

Leaders are responsible for building organizations that are engaged fully with their internal and external environments so that they are able to take on opportunities. Their style

92 Mancheno-Smoak, L., Endres, G. M., PhD., Polak, R., & Athanasaw, Y., "The individual cultural values and job satisfaction of the transformational leader." *Organization Development Journal*, 27(2009):9-21. Retrieved from http://0-search.proquest.com.library. regent.edu/docview/198046012?accountid=13479. p.10.

93 ibid, 17.

of leadership influences how they interact with followers. A transformational style encourages the development of a strong relationship with followers. Such an engaged leader-follower relationship will ultimately help design and implement the means to increase the effectiveness of a company's ability to connect with the external environment.

This transformational leadership preference is evident in low masculinity and high femininity societies.[94] Such leaders tend to be more encouraging at heart, inspiring a shared vision and to modelling the way. They believe in recognizing individual contributions and strengthening the team through harmony and compassion for the well-being of others. They exhibit a passion for people. Leadership in masculine cultures, on the other hand, only becomes a tool of capital's advance.[95] More individualistic employees will prefer a transactional relationship to an affective linkage.[96]

Having inspirational leaders is the first step to developing resilient companies. Those in Asia in the current context now understand what it takes to change effectively by first building the foundation of the business, which is the people. With individuals in a company aligned and in-sync with each other in terms of values, mission and purpose, the business understands its capacity when it undergoes any change

---

94 Mancheno-Smoak et.al., *Cultural*, 17.

95 Piterman, *Leadership*, 191.

96 Felfe, J., Yan, W., & Six, B., "The impact of individual collectivism on commitment and its influence on organizational citizenship behavior and turnover in three countries." *International Journal of Cross Cultural Management:CCM*,8(2008):211.Retrievedfromhttp://0-search.proquest. com.library.regent.edu/docview/221135245?accountid=13479. p.230.

initiative. Being able to move earlier and more effectively than its competitors today create a first-mover advantage. Leaders are able to inspire individuals by engaging and making them part of the whole change activity.

The second portion to the TriNodic Leadership Model is explored in the next two chapters. This model suggests that an organization should be structured in a way so that it is able to help people manage information and knowledge that are required for decision making.

The chapters will also explore decision-making in private and public organizations and how it can be improved. The combination of proper knowledge management and an organization that is decisive across its hierarchies allows it to be equipped to take on any change initiative that may be critical to get ahead of the competition.

> **Take Away Messages (Chapters 10-15)**
>
> - Leaders understand the pressure that the strive for profit, profit and profit (3Ps) when engaging with followers;
> - People understand "Me"/individualistic and "We"/collectivistic cultures and what these mean for leaders to engage with the employees;
> - The difference and impact of performance or relationship priority in the 3Ps culture;
> - Leaders appreciate the ideal leadership style suitable for 3P cultures.

Part

TRINODIC LEADERSHIP MODEL

03

Decisive
information system

Manage Information

The first part of the TriNodic Leadership Model focuses on the need for leaders to be inspirational because they inspire, engage and encourage individuals to change to contribute to their organization. In the previous chapters, we covered extensively about how leaders and employees/followers interact and why they behave the way they do. We even explored how this interaction could be improved in view of the pressure placed upon both of them in light of an environment today that focuses intensively on the 3Ps, especially in Asia. In this second section of the book, we explore the second part to the TriNodic Leadership Model. It explains how leaders must build and design a structure that is able to process information efficiently. This will help them make decisions and prescribe solutions to manage any changes and remain competitive.

Leaders and employees are constantly receiving information. This is on the external environment, internal conflicts, competitors and those that impact the future of the industry. This chapter deals with how an organization must be designed to ensure that such information is processed efficiently. Chapter 21 deals with how then to create a decisive organization where it can process information efficiently to reach at a level where decisions can be made quickly and appropriately.

Leaders must build companies that create environments with the ability to promote and introduce new developmental methods.[97] In our situation, this means having an entire structure with an information system that helps a company to make fast effective decisions, remain competitive and encourage innovation.[98] This will give it the capacity to respond quickly to pressures and be the predictor of business success.[99] A company must also be able to undergo structural modifications such as decentralization of making decisions.

Information that is analyzed includes knowledge collated from every aspect of a company.[100] This must stimulate everyone's participation and lead to enhancements and reduce ambiguities in the interpretation of data.[101] A company must also have the capability to adapt when provoked, even

---

97 Trebesch, S.G., "Developing Persons in Christian Organizations: A Case Study of OMF International." *The Journal of Applied Christian Leadership*, 2(2008): 27. p.28.

98 Ogbanna, E. & Harris, L.C., "Innovative organizational structures and performance: A case study of structural transformation to groovy community centers." *Journal of Organizational Change Management*, 16(2003): p.513.

99 ibid, 514.

100 Barboroux, P., "A design-oriented approach to organizational change: insights from a military case study." *Journal of Organizational Change Management*, 24(2011): 636.

101 Barboroux, *Design*, 636.

to the point of chaos, and emerge into a more complex and, often, higher performing entity.[102]

In today's rapidly changing economic and social environments, leaders must constantly be decisive in identifying and solving problems.[103] Many challenges demand decisions when there are no clear-cut criteria as issues are often neither repetitive or well defined.[104] A leader is then required to respond quickly and appropriately. This constant change even requires public sector bodies to undergo reforms that move the task of making decisions away from the central government to those closer to the people.[105] Before we discuss the topic about how to be a decisive organization, we need to first dwell into the realm of how information should be managed.

---

102 Englehardt, C.S. & Simmons, P.R., "Organizational flexibility for a changing world." *Leadership & Organization Development Journal,* 23(2002), 113.

103 Daft, *Organization*, 452.

104 Daft, *Organization*, 453.

105 Bhuiyan, S. H., & Amagoh, F., "Public sector reform in Kazakhstan: issues and perspectives." *International Journal of Public Sector Management,* 24(2011): 227-249. doi:10.1108/09513551111121356.

Design a Nimble, Sound Structure

Organizational design is described as the search for coherence between strategies, its mode and integration of individuals[106]. Galbraith (1977) defines six variables in design, namely task, structure, information, decision processes, reward system and people.[107] Companies today work in hypercompetitive environments and these conditions demand that they are able to adapt their structures and processes with great flexibility. In this sense, they must be able to change the way they design and distribute tasks and assign roles and responsibilities. And they must have the ability coordinate decisions and activities, while maintaining the integrity of their structures so that there is continuity in their actions.[108]

---

106 Galbraith, J.R., *Organization Design.* (Reading, MA: Addison-Wesley Publishing Company, 1977)
107 ibid, 31
108 Barbaroux (2011). p.626.

Managing the power of knowledge

For an organization to be decisive, the focus must not only be on delegating or empowering employees increase its capacity to so. It must also be designed to manage information. Knowledge is power in today's economy and when it is integrated into a management structure, a company is able to anticipate and take on the future with confidence. Design, then, plays a key part in creating organizations that are innovative and engage with their environment because of their ability to handle information. This encourages confidence in a company to make the right decisions at all levels and takes away the tendency to micro-manage issues and put this in the hands of others.

A conventional company structure is the result of a combination of a few justifiable criteria. These include location of suppliers, customers and divisions, departments with different portfolios, variety of products and services, specialized employees and units dedicated for regulatory compliance.[109] Such companies evolve over time and the transformations they undergo tend to lead the sub-optimal capability for performance and growth. This often lacks focus on building pathways that encourage efficient knowledge management. Knowledge exchange is essential to maintaining effectiveness in a modern company where it is a key factor of production.[110]

---

109 Mahesh, K. & Suresh, J.K., "Knowledge criteria for organization design." *Journal of Knowledge Management*, 13(2009): 45.
110 ibid, 49.

Information intensity and complexity also place further demands on organizations and make them inefficient at predicting, spotting or responding to change.[111] The answer is to ease that exchange of knowledge. This refers to the existence of natural or culturally preferred situations that encourage constant interaction among people with similar interests. It entails preventing information getting entrenched in silos.[112]

Over and above the capacity to exchange knowledge, is the right people taking ownership of it. This ensures that those entrusted with it maintain and nurture the currency of their specialized areas of responsibility. This can be accomplished when they have an identity in the company's structure. Lastly, the organization must be able to convert some of its knowledge into intellectual properties in the form of patents, design registrations and publications. Special recognition, rewards, and review and authorization structures can ensure this is done effectively.

Leaders can create and give knowledge units prominence on existing conventional structures.[113] These units grow and nurture information in the area of their expertise. They bring together employees with common interest from across different business departments to collaborate. This hybrid structure work in both product and service-oriented organizations.

---

111 Englehardt & Simmons, *Flexibility*, 113.
112 Mahesh & Suresh. *Knowledge*, 46.
113 ibid, 47.

Build the Ideal
Knowledge Carriers

Access to knowledge and information forms the basis for making sound decisions. Information is the most valued asset in managing change especially in a competitive environment.[114] For any change in the public sector, knowledge management must be developed and applied at the national level.[115] By implementing knowledge management practices, a country needs to change their belief and behaviors pertaining to knowledge adoption and its associated benefits.[116] It requires a culture that engages people, who work together to develop, share and use the knowledge gained.

To share this effectively, there needs to be active participation by stakeholders. A community that recognizes globally accepted sharing practices facilitates this active participation.

114 Jafari, M., & Akhavan, P., "Essential changes for knowledge management establishment in a country: a macro perspective." *European Business Review*, 19(2007): 89-110. doi:10.1108/09555340710714162.
115 ibid, 91.
116 ibid, 101.

In public sectors, government policies, public belief and social awareness are important for this to take place.[117] In the private sector, an organization could look at its employees who are similarly aware to implement policies.

Leaders must create a sense of belonging, empowerment, trust, and respect, before people start to engage with each other. They have to build the right "carriers" to share knowledge, whether these are technologies, templates or models. But there must first be an effective infrastructure, as a technological medium to share and disseminate knowledge.

In the public sector, governments that build frameworks to encourage the sharing of knowledge, as in Malaysia through eGovernment, improve interaction with their citizens, who are then empowered with information.[118] Malaysians, for instance, are encouraged to participate in shaping, debating and implementing public policies.[119] Where there is greater participation, there is more collective ownership of what has been decided.[120] This promotes sustainable progress in the country.

In Zambia, where delivery of health services was decentralized to district levels, access to information was a powerful tool

---

117 ibid, 101.

118 Zhao, F., "Impact of national culture on e-government development: a global study." *Internet Research*, 21(2011): 362-380. doi:10.1108/10662241111139354.

119 Wong, K., Fearon, C., & Philip, G., "Understanding egovernment and egovernance: stakeholders, partnerships and CSR." *International Journal of Quality & Reliability Management*, 24(2007): 927-943. doi:10.1108/02656710710826199.

120 Wong, Fearon, & Philip, eGovernment, 940.

for local governments to improve the level of care for their people.[121] In Ukraine, the introduction of enterprise education help equip people with enterprising skills, behaviors and attributes for working in a market economy.[122] This tool empowers everyone in the community to manage change with information they have access to.[123] Enterprise education encourages new ideas and helps bring about economic and societal transition.[124] It offers people the potential to present new solutions to old problems with an educational framework around which cultural transformation can progress.

---

121 Kanyengo, C. W., "Contextualising library and information policies for health-care delivery in Zambia." *Library Review*, 58(2009): 685-689.

122 Jones, B., & Iredale, N., "Case study: international development in Ukraine." *Journal of Enterprising Communities: People and Places in the Global Economy*, 2(2008): 387-401. doi:10.1108/17506200810913935

123 ibid, 388.

124 ibid, 390.

Create and Store Knowledge

Intellectual capital is made up of human and knowledge resources.[125] The human side of this consists of talents and experts who acquire what they know through their education, training, experience and development. Knowledge capital documented information as a result of human capital. Managing intellectual capital builds a bridge between old and new ways of doing things. For the IT industry, this involves taking risks to learn and seek lasting solutions to problems instead of quick fixes.

Learning organizations as defined by Senge (1990) are those "which cannot learn because learning is so insinuated into the fabric of life". It involves a group of people who continually enhance the capacity to create their ideas. They focus on activities that gain knowledge from their experiences and those of others, and applying their expertise to fulfil their company's

---

125 Baines, A., "Exploiting organizational knowledge in the learning organization." *Work Study*, 46(1997): 202-206.

mission.[126] Baines (1997) highlights that the learning process is executed by marrying technology, organizational structures and cognitive-based strategies to raise the yield of existing knowledge. It also involves maximizing the potential of employees through self-development with the help of their company. The collective effort to exploit the ability to learn from experience and harness this also forms part of the continual improvement for an organization.

The result is the creation of new knowledge by acquiring, storing and utilizing it for learning, problem solving, and decision making. This will also result in fewer errors and duplication of effort, a quicker way to solve problems, improvements in making decisions, a reduction of research and development costs, increased worker independence, better customer relations and an enhancement in products and services.[127] Intellectual capital is the fundamental input to all creativity.[128] Innovation in an organization is also nourished and driven by knowledge-based capabilities, and management systems and processes that maximize their potential. Specifically, knowledge management investments also reduce the time for companies to enter new markets.[129] More on learning organizations will be covered in the third section of this book that connects such a culture and its capacity to businesses to also be future-centered.

---

126 Baines, *Knowledge*, 202.
127 ibid, 203.
128 ibid, 204.
129 Baines, *Knowledge*, 203.

20

Develop Human Capital

People make a company what it is. Developing them to manage information is critical for any company to be decisive. For example, IT start-ups typically undergo peculiar challenges ranging from product development to customer service delivery. They need to process massive amounts of information before making decisions, particularly on creating new products. IT start-ups depend to a large degree on human capital and developing a learning culture, especially on innovation, to generate as much relevant information as possible. These high-tech companies are dependent on knowledge workers, such as engineers, to exchange and combine information in new ways.[130] The competitive advantage in the IT industry is having employees who can create and manage knowledge to produce superior performance.[131] To develop them, a high percentage of their revenue is invested in research and development, and training to develop expertise to provide cutting-edge customer

---

130 Cho, Y., McLean, G.N., "Successful IT start-ups' HRD practice: four cases in South Korea." *Journal of European Industrial Training*, 33(2009): 134.
131 ibid, 127.

service.[132] These employees are often provided with bonus plans to hone their skills.

Caring, nurturing and sustaining the experience of its staff will give a company the ability to be alert to change and compete.[133] It must also have significant levels of flexibility and the ability to design and experiment. This will place a company in a state of frequent, nearly continuous change in structures, processes, and goals of its vision. Rowley & Gibbs (2008) champions that a learning organization is insufficient and that it should instead strive further to possess practical wisdom:

A practically wise organization is one that has a culture of concern for others such that individuals are inducted into a culture of deliberative action, to a praxis of practical wisdom where they learn by practical experience to becoming expert in making judgments initially within their specific domain based on the relative data but then in a more general sense to become experts at understanding the implication of data.[134]

An organization is required to understand universal issues it encounters and act on them.[135] It must embrace the uncertainty of its future by developing the competence and experience of those who make judgments. Rowley & Gibbs (2008) suggests that if a company were to be practically wise, it must possess the qualities of personal mastery and team learning. We suggest it also needs to learn from economic downturns.

---

132 Cho & McLean, *IT*, 134.
133 Baines, *Knowledge*, 204.
134 Rowley, J., & Gibbs,P., "From learning organization to practically wise organization." *The Learning Organization*, 15(2008): 356-372.
135 ibid, 364.

Challenging entrenched views

An organization must encourage employees to learn and accomplish goals with confidence in areas of interest to them.[136] Each employee has a mental model or worldview that is shaped by their upbringing, tradition, culture and values. The organization must aim to build a process whereby these views are challenged constantly in order to expose flaws in their mental models and to help them search for healthier alternatives.

Team Learning

To gain practical wisdom, a company must have supporting mechanisms that allow it to have a shared approach to problem-solving and conflict resolution.[137] This can only take place when the team shares clear, common goals and there is confidence in their respective competencies. The result of team learning is high performance and productivity. A shared vision is critical to move a company in one unified direction. This must be built upon the collective vision of its individual members through interaction and must not be forced upon them including that of its leader.

Learning from Recessions

Economic recessions threaten the survival of many start-ups.[138] All businesses, including established firms, respond

---

136 Baines, *Knowledge*, 205.

137 Baines, *Knowledge*, 205.

138 Latham, S., "Contrasting strategic response to economic recession in start-up versus established software firms." *Journal of Small Business Management*, 47(2009): 180-201.

to them differently. Smaller start-ups tend to be more adaptive and focus on revenue-generating activities, whereas larger firms rely on cost reductions in an effort to improve performance. Start-ups also increase investments in direct sales, alliances and channel efforts in contrast to their larger counterparts.[139] They are compelled to act on these areas to sustain market relevance among external third parties, such as customers.[140] These young firms increase their investments in the areas of research and development with more programmers and new products.[141] This is especially the case for technology companies as such investments are critical in their positioning strategy to gain a competitive advantage in the post-recessionary environment.[142]

Once an organization is structured to manage the information and knowledge, it must process them to arrive at useful decisions to make headway in its growth journey. In the next chapter, we will cover the structure necessary to make decisions efficiently that will ultimately drive an organization to be decisive by involving everyone across its hierarchy.

---

139 Latham, *Start-up*, 197.
140 Latham, *Start-up*, 196.
141 Latham, *Start-up*, 197.
142 Latham, *Start-up*, 197.

Take Away Messages (Chapters 16-20)

- Leaders must understand the importance of managing information when designing an organization that is capable of making good decisions;
- Individuals must explore how an organization can be built to encourage the generation and dissemination of information;
- Leaders must understand the need to develop the human capital to increase the engagement of all employees in managing knowledge.

Snip the Umbilical Cord

Ogbanna & Harris (2002) recommends that organizations be designed as "groovy community centers." They must also have a trendy, innovative and creative work environment where workers are empowered to tailor their activities toward satisfying the needs of their targeted communities, both internally and externally.[143] Performance indicators measure the effectiveness of these innovative designs.[144] The "groovy community centers" are characterized by a high level of decentralization, devolution of responsibilities and involvement in decision making.[145]

Innovative companies are often also able to strike a balance between budgets and schedules that have the flexibility to create innovative products and services according to the needs of the changing market.[146] Innovation is in opposition

---

143 Ogbanna & Harris, *Groovy*, 516.

144 ibid, 523.

145 ibid, 524.

146 Chanal, V., "Innovation management and organizational learning: a discursive approach." *European Journal of Innovation Management*, 7(2004): 56.

to persistence and change, or repetition and novelty. The strategy for innovative organizations is their ability to react to "hypercompetition". They are capable of creating permanent transformations while remaining continuously innovative through experimentation.[147] These organizations are continuously learning through complementary intra-project and inter-project ways. The social interactions inside a project, mainly based on conversations, constantly create and modify a shared repertoire of rules and resources.[148] These resources contribute to enrich work practices such as those creating a teamwork culture. To be able to achieve the above, companies must be designed to not only generate ideas and information that are revolutionary, but must ultimately arrive at decisions that will take them to the next level. In this chapter, we will cover how, today, they more than ever must be decisive and able to take affirmative actions that will allow them to excel in this competitive environment.

As a company grows, there is a need to be more flexible and have innovative units, but traditional patterns of thinking about control and accountability may hamstring it from doing this.[149] Decentralization gives the local unit power, control and autonomy so that it is able to flourish in its niches. This is essentially an action to cut off the umbilical cord. To enforce this separation, there must be consensus in five areas so that the central authority and the offshoot can

147 ibid, 57.

148 ibid, 63.

149 Morgan, G., *Imaginization: New mindsets for seeing, organizing and managing*. (Thousand Oaks, CA: Sage Publications, 2005): 74 (ISBN: 076191269X)

have a clear "cord agreement".[150] They span the overall vision and values, agreement on accountability, flow of resources in both directions, development of information systems for communication and rewards for achievements.[151]

---

150 ibid, 76.
151 ibid, 78.

Decentralization Key
to Growth

Often a company creates a centrally structured developmental program for any change that takes place in the initial stages.[152] In this situation, its key leaders create, design, implement, and infiltrate developmental ideas throughout the company. They form the values and outcomes of any change initiative. In addition, they hold regular meetings to set goals and hold the company accountable. Communication and training are also put in place in an orderly fashion to ensure initiatives are conducted in line with the company's vision and decision-making agenda. Having a marginalized department separate from the executive power of the central organization is seen to be unfavorable as it is unlikely to provide the leadership for initiatives it wants to roll out.

This structure presents challenges. Even in religious organizations in England, the church establishment had a

---

152 Trebesch, *Developing*, 54.

centralized structure. Their leaders had difficulty attending sessions for decision making unless they are given notice ample notice way in advance and are able to reserve those dates into their calendar.[153] This is why for a long time, the church in England faced difficulties in developing large-scale policies.[154] Centralization limits growth. Regional centers become liabilities because of their inability to be flexible and they cannot adapt quickly to their surroundings.[155] Size, as it grows, also becomes a barrier to flexibility.

At the simplest level, decentralizing decision making by delegating responsibilities to employees create a happier workplace. According to McDuff (2008), this and other concepts such as social integration and structural legitimacy in the workplace creates higher satisfaction and commitment from employees because they prize these values.[156]

Decentralization allows for increased participation in decision-making and autonomy, both of which are fundamental characteristics in professional work as they create satisfied employees who contribute willingly to the company.[157] Workers and their supervisors feel a sense of empowerment and are less likely to engage in behaviors that ultimately result in negative outcomes such as low job satisfaction and high turnover rates.[158] This is because the higher levels

---

153 Morris, B., "The Future of "High" Establishment." *Ecclesiastical Law Journal*, 12(2011): 271.
154 ibid, 273.
155 Morgan, *Imaginization*, 72.
156 McDuff, E., "Organizational Context and the Sexual Harassment of Clergy." *Sociology of Religion*, 69(2008): 301.
157 McDuff, Organizational, 301.
158 ibid, 302.

of autonomy due to the right structures provide both the motivation and mechanisms that followers need to deal effectively with any negative behaviors.[159] It, in turn, results in improved engagement between leaders and followers.

Decentralization in the public sector

Changes and reforms in the public sector are different from those in the private sector because they involve resolving conflicting interests or polarities.[160] In the public sector, these take place in a fishbowl where the agents of change are neither the biggest nor the most aggressive fish.[161] Such reforms involve negotiations and compromises where what is "right" is a matter of responding to various conflicts or polarities. Catering to various interests is not the common practice in the private sector where implementing strategies is the norm.[162]

Decentralization in the public sector involves the transfer of authority and responsibility from the central government to local authorities in areas of planning, management and decision making.[163] It is often about bringing the desire of politicians and policy makers closer to their constituents.[164] This can be territorial, functional or institutional in nature.

---

159 ibid, 311.

160 Cunningham, J. B., & Kempling, J. S., "Implementing change in public sector organizations." *Management Decision*, 47(2009): 330-344. doi: 10.1108/00251740910938948.

161 ibid, 330.

162 Cunningham & Kempling, *Implementing*, 330.

163 Regmi, K., Naidoo, J., Greer, A., & Pilkington, P., "Understanding the effect of decentralization on health services The Nepalese experience." *Management*, 24(2010): 361-382. doi:10.1108/14777261011064986.

164 ibid, 361.

It depends on geographical demarcation, the range of functions delegated and the way decision makers are recruited.[165] Decentralization takes on three different forms in public sector reform: political, administrative and fiscal.

i) Political

As we have pointed out, political decentralization empowers authorities down the food chain at the local level and they are accountable to constituents in their districts.[166] This results in an increase in public participation in decisions at that level and there is more transparency.[167]

ii) Administrative

This takes place when entities such as local level line-ministries and "street-level" agents yield power. They are accountable to the central government who appointed them as administrators at the local level and are extensions of the central state. They represent the central government to deliver services on its behalf.[168]

Privatization is another example of administrative decentralization. This often takes place to shift the cost of providing a service, such as education, from the state to the end users.[169] Often, it is in response to competition for public

---

165 ibid, 365.

166 Regmi, Naidoo, Greer, & Pilkington, *Decentralization*, 365.

167 Bhuiyan & Amagoh, *Kazakhstan*, 241.

168 Regmi, Naidoo, Greer, & Pilkington, *Decentralization*, 365.

169 Chan, D., & Tan, J., "Privatization and the rise of direct subsidy scheme schools and independent schools in Hong Kong and Singapore." *International Journal of Educational Management*, 22(2008): 464-487. doi:10.1108/09513540810895417.

funds from other public agencies. In the case of education, this tussle for funds usually results in a reduction of government expenditure.[170] Privatization brings about improved efficiency with more accountability to end-users.[171]

iii) Fiscal

The nature of this power transfer refers to the receipt of grants, imposition of fines and even tax.[172] For effective fiscal decentralization to take place there must be adequate provision of revenue from the central government and the proper delegation of powers to local authorities, especially in terms of expenditures.[173] It requires a design that produces the ability to contain cost with sufficient financial control.

The success of fiscal decentralization lies in the fact that local authorities have the capacity to generate increased revenue. In addition, decision makers are also physically accessible to beneficiaries at the local level, which means that they are able to exert effective pressure on the local government. The powers-that-be as a result becomes more progressive, responsive, and accountable to the people because of an improved dialogue among the state, citizens and communities.[174]

---

170 Chan & Tan, *Privatization*, 465.
171 ibid, 466.
172 Regmi, Naidoo, Greer, & Pilkington, *Decentralization*, 366.
173 ibid, 368.
174 Regmi, Naidoo, Greer, & Pilkington, *Decentralization*, 369.

Implement Reforms in Decentralization

In developing countries, central governments recognize that because of its expansive responsibilities, its administrators are not able to participate in all decision making effectively. Socio economic progress requires people's active participation and resource mobilization necessitates involvement at a local level. Decentralization is then a strategic policy to implement reforms. The devolution of power is also a precondition for a democratic model of governance.[175]

For example, with reforms in Singapore and Hong Kong, decentralization of decision-making no longer necessitates the government to carry out the work of coordinating education. The central government only needs to remain involved in regulating and delivering educational services.[176] There is a shift from total governmental control to an autonomous model that upholds different modes of accountability in different

---

175 Bhuiyan & Amagoh, *Kazakhstan*, 234.
176 Chan & Tan, *Privatization*, 484.

constituencies. In Singapore and Hong Kong, administrators switched from their traditional roles as professionals to that as chief executive officers. They became more proactive in dealing with changes as they are given more discretionary powers in financial matters and making decisions.[177] These organizations now have a managerial instead of professional accountability.

The central authority during the education reform strengthened the mechanisms of auditing and quality assurance in exchange for administrators having more managerial autonomy. In these privatized systems, the schools remain free to design their curricula, fee structures and even entrance requirements.[178] The increased autonomy stimulated educational innovation and allowed schools to respond more promptly and sensitively to the needs and aspirations of parents and students.[179]

Decentralization and autonomization of public-school systems in Korea and Taiwan include empowerment of stakeholders such as teachers and parents. They now have the opportunity to be involved and participate in the governance of schools.[180] This is in contrast to Singapore and Hong Kong where principals still play a dominant role in formulating education policies and school management.[181] South Korea and Taiwan

---

177 ibid, 468.

178 ibid, 469.

179 ibid, 471.

180 Lo, W. Y. W., & Gu, J. O., "Reforming school governance in Taiwan and South Korea: Empowerment and autonomization in school-based management." *International Journal of Educational Management*, 22(2008): 506-526.

181 ibid, 521.

went further where school principals and government only play roles as regulators and coordinators while parents and teachers exercise influence over school management. Nevertheless, decentralization in the school systems of these countries involves new participants in the operations of what are essentially public organizations.

Autonomy must devolve sufficiently for decentralization to be effective.[182] This is especially so with fiscal types. A country that could benefit from decentralizing its fiscal policy is Nepal, which bases its allocation of health budgets on incrementalism. This entails gradually increasing the previous years' figures that may not reflect the reality of actual needs and preferences of the local community. Best practices are not embedded as a necessary element to ensure that resources are allocated properly. In preparing budgets, the central authority may not utilize information from the local level to learn and design but as a way to extend more financial support.[183] Local preferences are, therefore, not incorporated into budgets.

---

182 Regmi, Naidoo, Greer, & Pilkington, *Decentralization*, 372.
183 Regmi, Naidoo, 372

24

Empower Local Authorities

In Kazakhstan, public reform through decentralization involves transforming the delivery of government's services at local levels. By granting powers and responsibilities to local authorities, citizens are able to participate in and help drive how decisions are made. This means local communities are then able to determine the services they want, according to their priorities.[184]

Local authorities make decisions on budgets, plans and programs, which they then finance. Decisions regarding the redemption of local debt, payment of interest on loans and maintenance of public order are also under their purview. They even decide on how to promote entrepreneurial activities in their market, such as research and development, and promotion of exports.

However, this restructuring of roles require an adherence to the rule of law.[185] In Kazakhstan, the President define the powers,

---

184 Bhuiyan & Amagoh, *Kazakhstan*, 235.
185 Bhuiyan & Amagoh, *Kazakhstan*, 235.

duties, rights and responsibilities of elected local authorities and their administrations. Their representatives and executive bodies are not allowed to make decisions that contradict with the national foreign, internal, financial and investment strategies.[186] In Nepal when the public health system was undergoing reform, there was similar reengineering of its district public healthcare services.[187] It involved redesigning the public health hierarchy, fiscal structure and the system of effective governance.

Increased Efficiency with Improved Governance

The objective of decentralization is to deliver good local governance and public service because it increases efficiency.[188] It makes public systems more equitable, inclusive and fair.[189] The result is an improvement of the public sector performance. Decentralization achieves this because it diminishes the problems that come with centralization, bureaucracy, inflexibility and corruption.[190] It makes public services more responsive to the needs of the people.[191]

In managing Brazil's Amazon region, the government's transfer of administration to authorities there empowers local communities, encourages greater participation from non-governmental organizations and redistributes financial

---

186 ibid, 236.
187 Regmi, Naidoo, Greer, & Pilkington, *Decentralization*, 362.
188 Bhuiyan & Amagoh, *Kazakhstan*, 235.
189 Regmi, Naidoo, Greer, & Pilkington, *Decentralization*, 361.
190 Regmi, Naidoo, Greer, & Pilkington, *Decentralization*, 364.
191 ibid, 365.

resources.[192] It also enhances cooperation between the public and private sectors.[193] As a result of decentralization it brought into existence a relatively permanent institutionalized arrangement composed of state, civil society and the private sector. They were given direct and indirect say in local and regional environmental matters to manage natural resources.[194] The local environmental governance model overcomes historical obstacles such as budgetary constraints, disrespect of the law, lobbying of interest groups, corruption, and the lack of political will to create a sustainable environment.[195]

In this second instalment to the TriNodic Leadership Model, we covered the importance of understanding that leadership involves leading an organization that is able to not only generate information and knowledge but also how information has to be managed. This allows any company to be receptive to what is taking place in its environment. Taking and understanding information and converting it into useful knowledge is insufficient in today's economic climate. The critical thing is not only to be able to manage knowledge but to help it make critical decisions at the right time. This steers and organization to be decisive on items that will have an impact on its future. This not only involves leaders at the top making quality decisions but also to empower everyone in an organization to do so. It creates efficiency and a conducive

---

192 Lima, I. B. D., & Buszynski, L., "Local environmental governance, public policies and deforestation in Amazonia." *Management of Environmental Quality: An International Journal,* 22(2011): 292-316. doi:10.1108/14777831111122888.
193 ibid, 301.
194 ibid, 302.
195 ibid, 308.

environment for them to engage and get involved in any change initiative.

In the next section of the book, we will explore the third portion of the TriNodic Leadership Model. It will cover and explain why an organization must adopt a strategic thinking mindset to help it remain ahead of the competition. It speaks extensively about how a company with strategic thinking, focused on the future, is able to do this. A company must understand the future it may have to face so that it is able to mitigate risks and prepare to take advantage of any opportunities it is able to predict. Armed with such knowledge, a business will be able to leapfrog its competitors and remain in front of the pack.

Take Away Messages (Chapters 21-24)

- Leaders must understand the importance of organizing a company so that it is able to make decisions across hierarchies;
- Leaders must understand that having a decentralized structure is key to making an organization become more decisive and responsive to its environment;
- The chapter uses the public sector as a case study of how decentralization has worked well to tackle the myriad of information it has to process constantly to arrive at decisions.

Part

TRINODIC LEADERSHIP MODEL

A future-centered strategy

04

Look Beyond the Horizon

Competition is more aggressive today. To adapt to this field of play and maintain the edge to thrive, leaders must map out a path for their companies that is not dependent on previous solutions.[196] They must lead their companies to always be "the early bird takes the worm". This means leaders must constantly be a few steps ahead of the competition to capture opportunities before anyone snatches them.[197] The goal, then, is to prepare their troops for what the future will throw at them in the next 10 to 15 years.

This entails identifying the drivers of change that will shape and take industries far into the horizon. Recognizing what these are will put them in a position to install systems that can paint a reliable picture of the likely scenarios that will come their way.

---

196 Ashley, W. C., & Morrison, J. L., *Anticipatory management: 10 power tools for excellence into the 21st century.* (Leesburg, VA: Issue Action, 1995). ISBN: 0913869058. p.3.
197 Ashley & Morrison, *Anticipatory*, 5.

What are these systems?

One such instrument is a network of information channels that points the way for an organization to learn constantly from the theatre it is operating in. Once in place, it will promote a culture among its employees to use critical intelligence that can make an impact on the organization at some point down the road. This will arm them with the right ammunition to face head on with the speed traps and fast zones that are on the highway to the future.

The next three chapters of the book touches on the third element of the TriNodic Leadership Model. It calls for leaders to be future-centric so that they can understand what is coming their way. Flushed with all the available information from their crystal balls, they can then have a clear picture of likely scenarios that will pop up and make the right calls for each of them. This insight is the light on the road they have to be on to help them to stay clear of potholes during downturns and grab the opportunities when the economy booms. Whatever the scenario may be, a company will be better prepared to deal with all sorts of situations because it understands what is in store in the future.

Ditch Ideas Stifling Innovation

Why are leaders today working harder and doing things faster? The answer is that they have not been exploring new ideas and are instead trying to make what they feel are their time-honored, but old, models work, which actually don't.[198] So-called years of experience are, in fact, what a typical organization goes through.[199] It is a myopic way of dealing with change[200].

What leaders must do, then, is to ditch old ideas that stifle innovation, the kind that strategic planning does in an attempt to systematize the workplace. [201] Under this formula, a leader only focuses on portions of the overall plan and is not motivated to deal with macro-world changes outside the

---

198 Ashley & Morrison, *Anticipatory*, 10.
199 Ashley & Morrison, *Anticipatory*, 10.
200 Ashley & Morrison, *Anticipatory*, 10.
201 Ashley & Morrison, *Anticipatory*, 25.

organization.[202,203] This method is no longer effective in this fast-paced era we are in and only analysts, rationalists and people who exalt logic, thrive in it.[204] Not innovators.

In casting our eyes far ahead of time, the correct tool is strategic thinking. This is a sharper instrument that encourages a talented manager to be creativity in the use of resources and assets at his disposal and to reinvent them with a fresh coat of paint.[205]

Strategic thinking involves a marriage of information and insight, and focuses on interrelationships rather than individual components. It views the surroundings of an organization not as a "snapshot" but a "moving picture"[206] that gives a leader a broader panoramic picture of key data including its stakeholders and competition. It gives him the tools to respond to situations through a comprehensive set of initiatives.[207]

Armed with reliable information, a leader is able to produce, analyze and prioritize bold and imaginative ideas. He can then share the potentially successful ones with everyone in the organization.[208]

---

202 Ashley & Morrison, *Anticipatory*, 27.
203 Ashley & Morrison, *Anticipatory*, 31.
204 Ashley & Morrison, *Anticipatory*, 25.
205 Ashley & Morrison, *Anticipatory*, 26.
206 Ashley & Morrison, *Anticipatory*, 35.
207 Ashley & Morrison, *Anticipatory*, 35.
208 Ashley & Morrison, *Anticipatory*, 37.

Keep an Eye on
the Future

The future is thought of as clusters of possibilities, not probabilities or certainties.[209] It is rooted in the past and the present, and this is at the heart of thinking strategically.[210] Foresight, where the focus is on the future, is a component of this. It is a set of activities that gives a clearer picture of data that a network of information channels provides.[211]

When strategically integrated into an organization's structure, it acts as a bulwark against reactive responses to situations, which are often too late. Strategic foresight allows leaders to position resources in the right places to respond aggressively to opportunities when these open up for them. This is a sea change

---

209 Zepke, *Thinking*. N., "Thinking strategically in response to New Zealand's tertiary education strategy: The case of a Wananga." *Journal of Management and Organization*, 15(2009): 110-121.

210 Zepke, N., "Thinking strategically in response to New Zealand's tertiary education strategy: The case of a Wananga." *Journal of Management and Organization*, 15(2009): 110-121.

211 Solem, K. E., "Integrating foresight into government. Is it possible? Is it likely?" *Foresight*, 13(2011): 18-30. doi:10.1108/14636681111126229, 26.

from the traditional management style of simply employing the right skills and knowledge to answer challenges.[212]

The hard truth is that traditional hierarchical models must give way to newer, nimble designs.[213] To acquire these requires a revolutionary way of thinking. It calls for an organization to construct a positive image of the future, to anticipate not only the negative outcomes of their decisions but to maintain an ethos of positive expectations.[214]

So how does a leader help an organization gain the ability to have foresight? An indispensable part of this process is called "futuring".

This takes the form of brainstorming ideas[215] but goes beyond discussing random proposals. Futuring sit-downs shift into a visionary mode that challenge assumptions, know what needs to change and what not to, have contingency plans and action lists.

Continuity makes futuring possible, but rapid change requires acting out these plans with a degree of urgency.[216] It pushes an organization to experiment with new ways of operating, making decisions without all the desired data and finally about institutionalizing the strategic thinking methodology as the new planning framework.[217]

---

212 Bishop & Hines, *Thinking*, 13.
213 Ashley & Morrison, *Anticipatory*, 26.
214 Bishop & Hines, *Thinking*, 15.
215 Bishop & Hines, *Thinking*, 106.
216 Cornish, *"Futuring"*, 211.
217 Bishop & Hines, *Thinking*, 223.

Futuring is one among several activities that gives an organization foresight and this is its primary goal. It does this by actively exploring future possibilities for the company to explore various response models.[218,219]

Ultimately, it gives a company the ability to develop strategic foresight that produces high quality views applicable to emerging insights.[220] In the case we are discussing here, it is about understanding what forces could impact the way a workforce changes how firms manage its employees.

Futuring consists of both quantitative and qualitative means to monitor signals, clues and indicators of evolving trends and developments.[221] The simplest of these techniques is trend analysis. Determining a trend entails identifying its origin, direction and some possible consequences.[222]

The second technique is scenario planning. This takes more time and effort to discover the cause of an event.[223] A depth in understanding the assumptions and perceptions that exist for each possible scenario is necessary.[224] This process calls for the creating of persuasive and credible stories to explain how the world works.[225]

---

218 Cornish, *"Futuring"*, 204.
219 Cornish, *"Futuring"*, 213.
220 Bishop & Hines, *Thinking*, 5.
221 Solem, *Foresight*, 26.
222 Solem, *Foresight*, 26.
223 Solem, *Foresight*, 26.
224 Solem, *Foresight*, 27.
225 Solem, *Foresight*, 27.

The third method is the Dephi technique that was developed in the late 1950s. It essentially allows results or judgments to be formed without influences from dominating or domineering leadership personalities. This method produces superior expert opinion that delivers better advice.[226]

---

226 Solem, *Foresight*, 27.

Keys to Unlock Future Map

Foresight is not only about being future-centered or understanding what might crop up in the distant horizon and the possible solutions to address them. There are tangible benefits and some of these are:

i) Guide for Policy Decisions

Foresight functions like a GPS in strategic thinking and planning, which are both complementary to each other.[227]

In the public sector, foresight helps planners steer clear of bureaucratic, financial and incremental tendencies in strategic planning.[228] In Rongping, Zhongbao, Sida, & Yan (2008), we see that the foresight action is closely tied to planning. It is not planning per se but a step within it.[229] A survey in Canada zooms in on its importance in informing

227 Zepke, *Thinking*.
228 Zepke, *Thinking*.
229 Rongping, M., Zhongbao, R., Sida, Y., & Yan, Q., "Technology foresight towards 2020 in China": the practice and its impacts." *Technology Analysis & Strategic Management*, 20(2008): 287-307. doi:10.1080/09537320801999587, p.288.

and guiding policy decisions.[230] Its role is not to define policy but to condition it to be more flexible or robust on a given situation.[231] Distancing foresight activities, away from the intrusiveness of day-to-day operations, allows for wider issues to be examined. It leads to a greater understanding of the larger external context. This comes about when, in cooperating with analysts, the role of decision makers is strictly supportive and their interest is only in the progress of strategic thinking.[232]

ii) Anticipate Emerging Risks

Foresight does this when proper methods and techniques are established and integrated.[233]

Too often, leaders can't manage risks and avoid doing so because they are unable to cope with rapid changes in the environment and the onset of new, global trends that occur simultaneously and with sudden strength.[234] The objective of foresight teams, therefore, is to spot opportunities for policy development. They help to shift the focus of individuals to emerging risks and opportunities and highlight unintended consequences of new proposals.[235] Foresight teams should project over a longer term, but this is subject to time horizons

---

230 Calof, J., & Smith, J. E., "Critical success factors for government-led foresight." *Science and Public Policy*, 37(2010): 31-40. doi: 10.3152/030234210X484784, p.31.
231 Solem, *Foresight*, 28.
232 Solem, *Foresight*, 28.
233 Solem, *Foresight*, 24.
234 Solem, *Foresight*, 24.
235 Leigh, A., "Thinking Ahead : Strategic Foresight and Government." *Australian Journal of Public Administration*, 62(2003):3-10, p.5.

that each different issue presents.[236] Leaders can achieve this if they explore risk environments actively in order to manage potential new hazards.[237]

iii) Faster Decisions

Foresight cuts through clutter to give decision makers a clear picture for them to take swift actions, whether to seize opportunities or tackle problems.

There are leaders who are focused on data generation and they are driven by a notion of efficiency. They strive to evaluate efficiency in quantitative terms, based on the amount of information at their disposal.[238] Such managers face an information overload that puts them at greater risk of delaying making important decisions and even postponing this vital task indefinitely.[239] They instead look at problems that are more easily understood and solved.[240] This will lead to planning that discounts the future and, unfortunately, with dire consequences.[241]

Decision makers must face head on problems that are complex, unclear and uncertain[242] and deciding which are the right solutions to address them is an important component for any company. Strategic thinking and a foresight culture embedded in an organization, can help leaders make sense

---

236 Leigh, *Thinking*, 5.
237 Leigh, *Thinking*, 5.
238 Solem, *Foresight*, 25.
239 Solem, *Foresight*, 25.
240 Solem, *Foresight*, 25.
241 Solem, *Foresight*, 25.
242 Solem, *Foresight*, 25.

of information by systematically dealing with it and making the necessary connections in a structured manner. This can be done by an incorporated and anticipatory framework that is in place, which we will cover more extensively in the next chapter.

iv) Enhances Competitiveness

Technology is an indispensable asset for any organization to remain relevant in the marketplace. Governments use technology foresight to develop specializations so that their respective countries can compete globally.[243] Studies on this provide them with conditions "for reflections to identify potential strategic moves that keep track with change on a social, technical and economic level."[244] This involves scanning for the most suitable coordinated system of players and variables which could influence or impact a desired future.[245]

In Taiwan, technology foresight have helped policy makers understand how to improve complex networking relationship while developing long-term economic growth.[246] A study by Su, Lee, & Yuan (2010) shows that foresight activities in general aim to promote national competitiveness in the global technology race and that no country can afford to be left

---

243 Riedy, C., "The influence of futures work on public policy and sustainability." *Foresight*, 11(2009): 40-56. doi:10.1108/14636680910994950, p.44.

244 Antunes, A., & Canongia, C., "Technological foresight and technological scanning for identifying priorities and opportunities: the biotechnology and health sector." *Foresight*, 8(2006):31-44. doi:10.1108/14636680610703072, p.31.

245 Antunes & Canongia, *Technological*, p.32.

246 Su, H.-N., Lee, P.-C., & Yuan, B. J. C., "Foresight on Taiwan nanotechnology industry in 2020." *Foresight*, 12(2010): 58-79. doi:10.1108/14636681011075713, p.59.

behind.[247] In today's China, the government conducts similar programs because globalization has accelerated the rapid development of high technology, which has created not only cooperation but also competition.[248]

Technology foresight is acknowledged as a process, "by which one comes to a fuller understanding of the forces shaping the long-term future which should be taken into account in policy formulation, planning and decision-making."[249]

---

247 Su, Lee, & Yuan, *Foresight*, 61.
248 Rongping, Zhongbao, Sida, & Yan, *Foresight*, 287.
249 Rongping, Zhongbao, Sida, & Yan, *Foresight*, 288.

Anticipate Opportunities

An organization's ability to learn is key to its success (De Kluyver & Perarce, 2009). How does a company cultivate this culture? A strategic thinking framework with its attending structures must first be in place. Part of this journey is to have a system that anticipates possible scenarios that must be confronted. It does this by keeping tabs on the external environment, which gives an organization the eyes to identify and take advantage of every new opportunity that shows up. This is about getting ready today to prepare for tomorrow. The next chapter will cover this anticipatory framework extensively.

The learning strategy

A learning culture that is second nature in its ranks puts a company on a firm footing to employ successful strategies to adapt to changes in its theatre of operations. This is because employees are able to recognize the rewards that come from the "change strategies" decision of their leaders. The opposite is true when there is no learning culture as they lack the information of what is taking place in their environment. It results in a situation where leaders and staff, who fear uncertainty, don't see eye to eye on why change strategies are needed for a company to survive.[250]

A learning culture fosters sustainable change actions in response to new situations.[251] According to Crossan and Bedrow (2003), learning "is a process in which an organization seeks to acquire information, knowledge, and/or capabilities so as to enhance its ability to operate and compete in the market".

In other words, organizations with high levels of learning capabilities are open to new ideas and more committed to new ways of doing things.[252] They face far less resistance and as an added benefit, learning becomes a mechanism against inertia.[253] Ultimately, the time needed to implement and manage change strategies is speeded up.[254]

Learning the clan way

A chain reaction kicks in when a company learns together. It acquires, distributes, interprets and retains this knowledge as an organizational memory (Huber 1991). The wealth of

---

250 Daft, *Organization,* 435

251 Chaiporn, V. and Amonrat, T., "Strategic change and firm performance: the moderating effect of organisational learning," *Journal of Asia Business Studies,* 5(2011)2: 194-210, p.200.

252 Chaiporn and Amonrat, *Strategic,* 200.

253 Tripsas, M. and Gavetti, G., "Capabilities, cognition, and inertia: evidence from digital imaging." *Strategic Management Journal,* Vol.21 (2000) Nos 10-11: 203.

254 Chaiporn and Amonrat, *Strategic,* 203.

experience gained and accumulated can then be articulated clearly and codified.[255]

But how do you build a solid learning culture in a company? It has to be organic.[256] This means there must be shared responsibility, flexibility, communication and coordination among every member of the company. Like a clan, they are inter-dependent and strive for mutual development.[257] This is not something that is evident in a place where things run mechanically and in a centralized manner.[258]

Knowledge is a key resource and managing it efficiently is key to a company's ability to keep its competitive advantage.[259] And when it can transfer knowledge across business units it will be in a position to execute change strategies successfully.[260]

A clan culture can break down barriers that impede the creation and sharing of knowledge assets.[261] It promotes a workplace where people share a lot about themselves and are team players who are highly committed to the company and

255 Zollo, M and Winter, S.G., "Deliberate learning and the evolution of dynamic capabilities." *Organisation Science*, 13(2002)3: 339-51.

256 Rebelo, T. M., & Gomes, A. D., "Conditioning factors of an organizational learning culture." *Journal of Workplace Learning*, 23(2011): 173-194. doi:10.1108/13665621111117215, p.185.

257 Rebelo and Gomes, *Conditioning*, 185.

258 Rebelo and Gomes, *Conditioning*, 185.

259 De la vega, A.F.R d Stankosky, M., "Knowledge management and innovation: what must governments do to increase innovation?" *Journal of Knowledge Management Practice*, 7(2006)4.

260 Cohen and Levinthal, *Absorptive*.

261 Suppiah, V., & Sandhu, M. S., "Organisational culture's influence on tacit knowledge-sharing behavior." *Journal of Knowledge Management*, 15(2011): 462-477. doi:10.1108/13673271111137439, 465.

co-workers. This attitude is displayed across the company from leaders to the rank and file. In such a workplace there is also a high propensity to share and make tacit knowledge accessible to everyone.[262]

Tacit knowledge is an asset that is "inarticulable" but intuitive and is a part of a person's cognitive thought and perception[263]. It makes up 90 percent of the knowledge of an organization.[264] Nonaka and Takeuchi (1995) state that, "Tacit knowledge is personal, context, specific and difficult to formalize and communicate". It is not easily shared using conventional mediums such as databases, systems and processes[265]. But it is developed directly from experience, and action.[266]

---

262 Suppiah and Sandhu, *Knowledge*, 471)
263 Suppiah and Sandhu, *Knowledge*, 462
264 Suppiah and Sandhu, *Knowledge*, 464
265 Suppiah and Sandhu, *Knowledge*, 464
266 Nguyen and Mohamed, *Leadership*, 207.

Transformational vs Transactional Leadership

So, what caliber of leaders brings out the best from employees for the ideal learning culture to thrive? Leadership is about managing relationships.[267] Today's leaders are expected to create a climate in which their followers are able to acquire knowledge that will allow them to adapt to changed strategies.[268]

Productive learning environments lead to innovative ways to solve problems and this increases the chances for an organization to be successful.[269]

The key is leadership style that reinforces the beliefs and values of a learning organization.[270] This and organizational

---

267 Retna, K. S., & Ng, P. T., "Communities of practice: dynamics and success factors." *Leadership & Organization Development Journal*, 32(2011): 41-59. doi:10.1108/01437731111099274, 51.
268 Nguyen and Mohamed, *Leadership*, 208.
269 Rebelo and Gomes, *Conditioning*, 174.
270 Retna and Ng, *Communities*, 51.

culture are two sides of the same coin[271] because while leaders shape cultural traits that reflect his or her own values and beliefs, [272] culture molds an organization's actions, beliefs, and values.[273]

There are two leadership styles that produce different outcomes.

The first is transformational that focuses on devising vision, shared values and ideas to build relationships.[274] This approach inspires trust, loyalty and admiration in followers, who would then subordinate their individual interests to the rest of the group's.[275]

Transformational leadership builds intangible qualities, such as vision-shared values, and ideas to build relationships in which followers become team players in the change process.[276] Employees are also motivated to be inquisitive and involved in taking intelligent risks, and to share their learning journey with colleagues.[277]

This management style frequently changes the organizational culture so that leaders and followers have mutual interests and a sense of interdependence.[278] When there is a need for followers to adapt to the organizational culture and realign

---

271 Nguyen and Mohamed, *Leadership*, 209.
272 Nguyen and Mohamed, *Leadership*, 209.
273 Nguyen and Mohamed, *Leadership*, 209.
274 Nguyen and Mohamed, *Leadership*, 208.
275 Nguyen and Mohamed, *Leadership*, 208.
276 Nguyen and Mohamed, *Leadership*, 208.
277 Nguyen and Mohamed, *Leadership*, 208.
278 Nguyen and Mohamed, *Leadership*, 209.

it with a new change or vision, transformational leadership behavior is necessary.

The second is transactional that rewards desired behaviors and the completion of tasks.[279] This leadership approach results in the compliance of followers but is unlikely to generate enthusiasm and commitment to their tasks.[280]

This type of leadership works to reinforce current management procedures by following existing norms, values and procedures.[281] When this is the focus, leaders can then devote time and resources to knowledge activities and issues, choosing to display behaviors that send a clear message that knowledge management is important.[282]

Ultimately, a fine balance must be found between the transformational and transactional leadership styles to create a successful knowledge management system.[283]

---

279 Nguyen and Mohamed, *Leadership*, 208.
280 Nguyen and Mohamed, *Leadership*, 208.
281 Nguyen and Mohamed, *Leadership*, 218.
282 Nguyen and Mohamed, *Leadership*, 218.
283 Nguyen and Mohamed, *Leadership*.

Take Away Messages (Chapters 25-30)

- There is a need to understand the importance and benefits of future centeredness in building a resilient organization that is able to understand the possible challenges and also opportunities that the future presents;
- Leaders need to integrate strategic thinking as part of being future centered;
- Leaders need to incorporate a continuous learning culture that allows the company to be staffed with strategic thinkers;
- The building of an anticipatory framework allows an organization to generate useful information. This continuous learning culture will ultimately also encourage the organization to be future centered;
- Understand the particular leadership style that is conducive to building a learning culture in organizations.

Futuring with a Crystal Ball

If given a chance to peek into the future, most people will grab it. Humans are curious animals and have a deep desire to know outcomes before they take place because we want the ability to prevent unfortunate events. But the crystal ball doesn't exist.

Yet, this reality does not mean we can't devise ways to see what the future might look like. It can mean the difference between success and failure. This is how companies gain foresight with a good degree of reliability. They hire talents who study trends and then paint a picture of what lie in the distant horizon. Armed with reliable intelligence, leaders can then plan, position and execute successful change strategies to good effect.

To achieve this, the leaders of tomorrow must be competent in maintaining a strong alignment with their followers and a culture that is conducive to change strategies. They also need to understand the importance of knowing what possible futures lie in wait.

Unless one has a crystal ball, the best any leader can do is to only anticipate likely scenarios and not predict them. This intricate process involves building the organization into a continuous learning machine.

An organization must also understand the importance to constantly monitor the external environment and if it does, then, a proper anticipatory framework has to be integrated into its structure. This will ensure that the futuring process becomes part of the business-as-usual practice with the same degree of importance as other functions such as sales, human resource management, technology, finance and other functions.

Before discussing what the integration of an anticipatory framework entails, we must first identify the right team of people to carry out this process.

The Strategic Leadership Team

Strategic leadership thinks, acts and influences in ways that promote an organization's sustainable competitive advantage.[284] To acquire such leaders the first step is to identify a Strategic Leadership Team (SLT), whose work has important implications on a business unit, product, service area, functional area, division and company.[285] A key attribute that qualifies a person to be part of the SLT is that his work contributes to long-term success.[286]

So, to build an organization that can execute change strategies effectively, a leader must do the following that examine:

- The current state of the organization that the Conducting Strategic Team Review and Action Tool (STRAT) shows; and

---

284 Hughes & Beatty, *Strategic*, 9.
285 Hughes & Beatty, *Strategic*, 167.
286 Hughes & Beatty, *Strategic*, 167.

- The possible challenges the organization will face in the future that an anticipatory framework is able to indicate.

Once the SLT has been formed, the organization then employs STRAT to identify the current state of the organization by determining the SLT members' effectiveness.

STRAT is designed to assess a strategic leadership team and their effectiveness. It consists of questions related to how the team functions, the members' leadership qualities and how they interact with each other. STRAT's objective is to generate conversations among SLT members to discover areas they are satisfied with as a team and allow them to look into areas where they can do better.[287]

They are required to rate areas related to the team's overall effectiveness.[288] But this should not be treated like a score board in which the aim is to outscore each other.[289] Such reviews are meant to periodically assess an SLT's ability to fulfil its role. It typically examines areas that include:

1. Assessing where the SLT is at;
2. Understanding what the SLT is and desired direction;
3. Learning how to get to the desired state; and
4. How to make the journey through the operational plans that have been set.

---

287 Hughes & Beatty, *Strategic*, 237.
288 Hughes & Beatty, *Strategic*, 191.
289 Hughes & Beatty, *Strategic*, 237.

Get Rid of Foxholes

Once the SLT members are identified, an anticipatory management process (AMP) system can be built to forecast the future. AMPs foster strategic thinkers who don't make the final call but provide decision makers with solid data to do so, including analyses of the external environment that will have an impact on the organization.[290]

Many companies apply concepts of statistical quality control, cross-functional work teams, empowered work groups and customers to deal with change. These, though, are insufficient.

AMP enhances this process and is systematic in calculating the disruptive impact of change and what solutions are needed.[291] It recognizes the doctrine that customers are important is no longer enough but what is important to them is.[292]

---

290 Ashley & Morrison, *Anticipatory*, 203.
291 Ashley & Morrison, *Anticipatory*, 207.
292 Ashley & Morrison, *Anticipatory*, 207.

Linking Anticipatory Management to the Organization

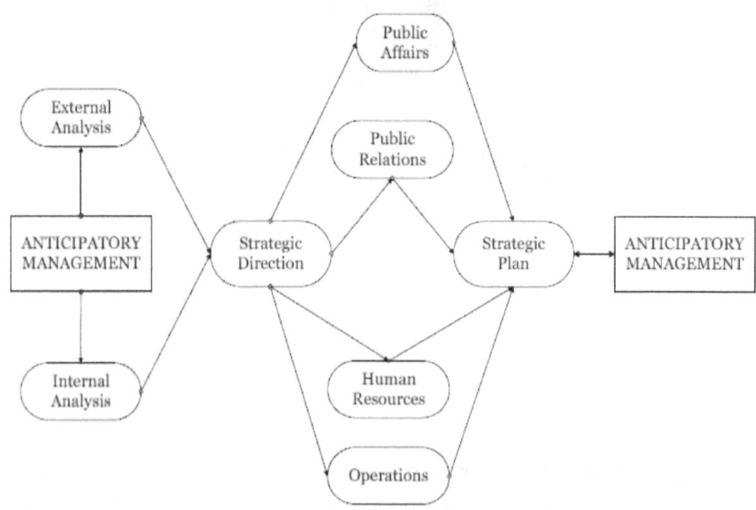

Source: Ashley, W. & Morrison, J. (1995). *Anticipatory management: 10 power tools for achieving excellence into the 21st century.* Leesburg, VA: Issue Action Publishing.

AMP addresses another significant problem that have weighed down many organizations plagued with a foxhole mentality. In this flawed approach, the practice is to break down a problem into various pieces. They are then given out to various departments to fix their respective bits. Each deal with their part of the problem, offering solutions based on their individual perspectives without the big picture in sight.[293] What happens as a consequence of this is that managers are isolated in their respective foxholes. Their modus operandi is survival of the fittest and their performances are rated accordingly.[294]

---

293 Ashley & Morrison, *Anticipatory*, 209.
294 Ashley & Morrison, *Anticipatory*, 209.

Such organizations are trained to function with little concern of getting caught in windy conditions. It requires intense concentration and this hinders the best and most committed managers to detect any incremental changes in the weather.[295] The data they receive is only used to reinforce their CEO's direction for the company. They are unable to act on conflicting intelligence until it's too late.[296]

AMP, on the other hand, breaks down artificial boundaries and prevent foxholes from appearing[297]. It positions an organization above these silos so that its members can peer over enemy lines to collect intelligence and manage uncertainty.[298]

This method brings attention to external issues that could affect their areas of responsibility and as a consequence foster cross-department dialogue.[299]

---

295 Ashley & Morrison, *Anticipatory*, 214.
296 Ashley & Morrison, *Anticipatory,,* 215.
297 Ashley & Morrison, *Anticipatory*, 217.
298 Ashley & Morrison, *Anticipatory*, 218.
299 Ashley & Morrison, *Anticipatory*ibid, 215.

Face the Future Head On

A MP has several tools at its disposal to do a competent job.[300] These include a Strategic Trend Intelligence System (STIS), Scenario Analysis, and Issue Life Cycle and scanning and monitoring assets. The first task of AMP is to identify emerging trends and challenge assumptions under which an organization operates.[301] Once this is done, the next step is to prioritize the information so that they form a checklist of actions to take in their respective degrees of their importance. This puts an organization in an ideal position to face the future head on.

---

300 Ashley & Morrison, *Anticipatory*, 191.
301 ibid, 59.

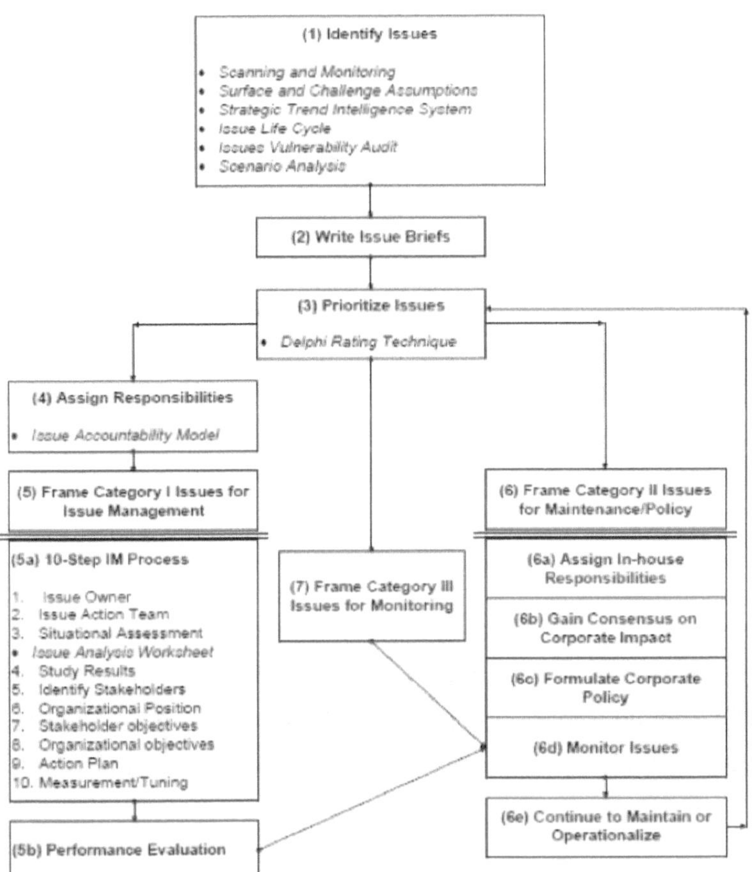

Source: Ashley, W. & Morrison, J. (1995). *Anticipatory management: 10 power tools for achieving excellence into the 21st century*. Leesburg, VA: Issue Action Publishing.

1. Identify Emerging Trends

Four tools in the AMP's armory scan the external environment of an organization to collect intelligence to help leaders prioritize actions on a range of foreseeable events. This is a big step in curating information on an organization's journey towards becoming a learning force.

How AMP works

Just as fishermen out in the deep sea select fish caught in their nets that can be sold and return to the waters those they can't, the practice of curating intelligence is similar. In scanning a range of data in the horizon, AMP does this work efficiently.

But it does more than just sifting for high value information. It also tracks new forces that are significant trends and then paints likely scenarios that can impact a company at either an industry or macro level.[302] All of this is done while considering an organization's operating structure to determine if it is resilient to the assumptions the AMP has churned out and if modifications are needed to make sure it can.

Armed with this information, the leadership then needs to confirm if these forces are indeed new trends that alter existing assumptions and have to use this data for their strategic plans. It will help them to maximize opportunities in the coming decade.

STIS

The job of constructing scenarios, based on curated intelligence, belongs to STIS or Strategic Trend Intelligence System. But the quality of the scenarios is only as good as its ability to scan and track trends for high-grade information.[303] Once STIS is able to identify the driving forces that could dislocate an industry, an organization uses this data to kick start the process of drawing up four likely future

---

302 Ashley & Morrison, *Anticipatory*, 60.
303 Ashley & Morrison, *Anticipatory*, 59.

scenarios.[304] These are then used to challenge its existing internal capabilities, before mobilizing resources to make the necessary adjustments to seize and maximize opportunities that have been identified.

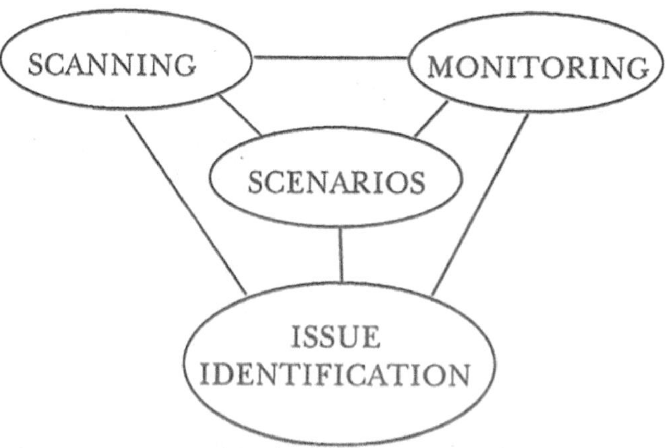

Source: Ashley, W. C., & Morrison, J. L. (1995). *Anticipatory management: 10 power tools for excellence into the 21*[st] *century.* Leesburg, VA: Issue Action. ISBN: 0913869058

---

304 Ashley & Morrison, *Anticipatory*, 214.

The Wind Tunnel Test

Planning scenario in 5 phases

Learning faster than your competitor delivers the ultimate competitive advantage (Chermack, 2011).[305] A strategy that takes its cue from STIS-driven scenarios is in essence a method of learning and unlearning.[306] In planning scenarios, decision makers recognize that uncertainty is a basic feature of organizational environments. When they acknowledge this reality and the problematic assumptions of a stable environment, these issues must be factored into the planning process. Leaders then have to search for alternative solutions.[307]

Chermack (2011) proposes that scenario planning has five phases:

---

305 Chermack, T. J., *Scenario planning in organizations: How to create, use, and assess scenarios.* (San Francisco, CA: Berrett-Koehler, 2011). ISBN 978-1605094137, p.xiii.
306 Chermack,, *Scenario*, xiii.
307 Chermack, *Scenario*, xv.

Phase 1: Project Preparation: Understanding Purpose and Building Rapport;

Phase 2: Scenario Exploration: Breathing in;

Phase 3: Scenario Development: Digging Deeper;

Phase 4: Scenario Implementation: Putting Scenarios to Use; and

Phase 5: Project Assessment: Documenting Results

Phases 1 - 3

The first two phases consist of having a scenario team in place, setting timelines, defining the scope of the project, and conducting trend and SWOT analyses, as well as the dynamics of the internal and external environments. Then, strategic conversations take place before an organization is ready to go on to Phase 3 of creating scenarios, which kicks off with a brainstorming workshop. This is where participants consider the major forces their organization is likely to face on a given issue.[308]

These forces are then ranked from "Low" to "High" to separate the critical factors from those that are not. The high-impact items are those that have the power to fundamentally reshape their business.[309]

All items are also ranked in terms of their degree of uncertainty. Those rated high for impact, form the critical issues that are used to plot scenario matrices as two independent variables.[310]

---

308 Chermack, *Scenario*, 133.
309 Chermack, *Scenario*, 136.
310 Chermack, *Scenario*, 141.

The latter will form the basis to develop four scenario stories – with at least one outline that is status quo while the rest are genuine alternatives.[311] The storylines must be relevant, challenging, and plausible without the possibility of being dismissed as improbable.[312] Once the three phases are completed the scenario planning work becomes a customized learning project for the organization.[313]

Phases 4 – 5

Chermack (2011) proposes that an organization be subjected to a wind tunnel test to examine the strategy, culture, capabilities and Business Idea of the organization.[314] It includes investigating key aspects in relation to the scenarios:

1. Whether the organization has viable strategies to support each possibility;
2. Whether the existing structure supports this type of organization;
3. Whether the current culture is an asset or liability;
4. What the status is of the human resource capabilities to maintain the Business Idea and whether there is the leadership capacity to manage the challenges.

Heijden (2005) proposes that we can test an organization's readiness in various scenarios by examining its internal and external perspectives.[315] The first looks at the organization's

---

311 Chermack, *Scenario*, 144.
312 Chermack, *Scenario*, 159.
313 Chermack, *Scenario*, 171.
314 Chermack, *Scenario*, 182.
315 Heijden, K. A. v. d., *Option planning. In Scenarios: The art of strategic conversation.* (Hoboken, NJ: John Wiley, 2005): 273.

capabilities to see if it can survive and flourish in the multiple equally plausible future environments they may face. The external outlook examines if the business is being developed in the right territory, considering the environments it may encounter.[316]

The Business Idea expresses the basis of the organization's overall competitive strength and growth principle.[317] It must be subjected to various scenarios to examine whether it continues to create customer value/cost leadership. It involves looking into the distinctive competencies of the organization.

Next, portfolio options should be considered. These can be developed through internal development, joint ventures, acquisitions or mergers.[318] They can either be investments in organic growth through expansion into similar markets or market share or spreading the Business Idea across a wider range of products. Another option is to look into investments in growth through partnerships, joint ventures or acquisitions by divesting into similar markets or expanding into different but closely related markets.

Capability options for any new Business Idea needs to start at examining those core competencies an organization already possesses. The leadership must then consider what other new generative distinctive competencies they need for a new product idea or what can be leveraged upstream or downstream through investments and partnerships or acquisitions. There may also be a consolidation or reformulating of existing

---

316 Heijden, *Option*, 273.
317 Heijden, *Option*.
318 Heijden, *Option*.

businesses.[319] Internal capabilities could include examining the financial and physical assets, human resources and the managerial support needed to manage each of the possible scenarios.

Assessing effectiveness

Assessing scenario planning projects is critical not only to understand the effectiveness of strategic activities but also to lend credibility to the process.[320] The goal is to present methods to estimate their benefits. This is accomplished through evaluating participant and stakeholder satisfaction by measuring the improvements in participant knowledge, expertise, systems and financial improvements.

---

319 Heijden, *Option*.
320 Chermack, *Scenario*, 212.

What's the Issue?

The Life Cycle of an Issue and Molitor's Model of Change

When businesses do not engage in anticipatory planning, their ability to define an issue, set an agenda and establish limits are limited.[321] Business leaders are often uncomfortable in dealing with vague concepts. A trend, issue and driving force for change are often ignored because there does not exist an easily recognizable path that tackles the bottom line.[322] As a result, business leaders have trouble agreeing on what issues to put on the agenda.[323]

---

321 Ashley & Morrison, *Anticipatory*, 81.
322 Ashley & Morrison, *Anticipatory*, 82.
323 Ashley & Morrison, *Anticipatory*, 82.

Molitor's Model of Change Theory

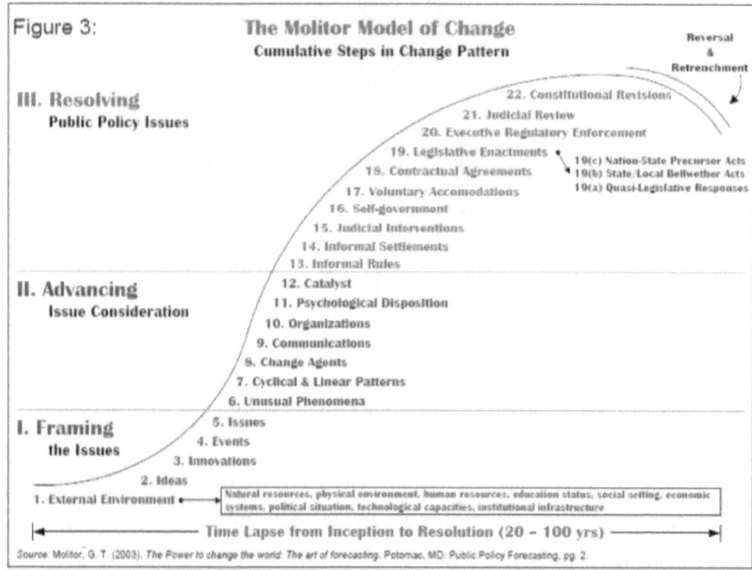

Life Cycle of an Issue

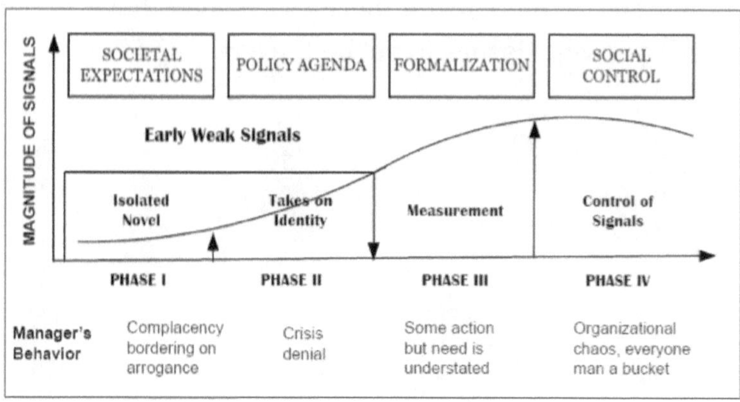

Source: Ashley, W. & Morrison, J. (1995). *Anticipatory management: 10 power tools for achieving excellence into the 21*[st] *century.* Leesburg, VA: Issue Action Publishing.

Organizations can use the Molitor Model of Change to anticipate emerging trends as the stages of an issue correspond to the life cycle that reacts to shifts in the external environment.[324] Ashley & Morrison (1995) divides the issue life cycle into four phases: societal expectations, policy agenda, formalization and social control. Innovators put forward their ideas and concepts in the first stage and are encouraged to allow them to mature.[325] Most ideas emanate from a gifted few but these can also flow from individuals through their practical experience.[326] Such ideas are posed as unproven hypothesis, where enhancements and refinement will follow.[327]

This usually takes place in Phase 2, which is policy agenda. At this stage, issues are allowed the opportunity for intervention but limited to modifying, rephrasing, or opposing the content of the initiative or issue.[328] At this stage, change agents champion the changes, with the organization providing the rallying points and curating deliberations through all forms of communications to create widespread awareness and understanding. This whole process will have the participation of catalysts. They arouse and enrage popular attitudes that ratchet up the process along while individuals seek ways to cope with change that directly impinges their situation.[329]

---

324 Ashley & Morrison, *Anticipatory*, 85.
325 Molitor, G. T., "Molitor Forecasting model: Key dimensions for plotting the 'patterns of change." *Journal of Future Studies*, 8(2003, August): 61-72. http://www.jfs.tku.edu.tw/8-1/A06.pdf, p.63.
326 Molitor, *Forecast*, 63.
327 Molitor, *Forecast*, 64.
328 Ashley & Morrison, *Anticipatory*, 87.
329 Molitor, *Forecast*, p.2.

By Stage 3, the issue has formalized and policies for the change have begun to be implemented. It is more a question of enforcing techniques, resolving an issue and how codes of ethics or rules of behavior are used to set the house in order.[330] This effectively leads to Stage 4 where public attention to the issue declines and compliance becomes costly. The whole process then starts anew because they are not satisfied with the change.[331] It is at this societal expectation phase that organizations should consider becoming involved where resources should be committed.[332]

Writing Briefs and Prioritising issues

While the issue is being identified, there is a need to sort all issues into either Category I consisting of items that require actions, Category II that do not need immediate action due to their maturity, or Category III for those do not need action.

---

330 Ashley & Morrison, *Anticipatory*, 88.
331 Molitor, *Forecast*, p.3.
332 Ashley & Morrison, *Anticipatory*, 87.

Issue Accountability Model

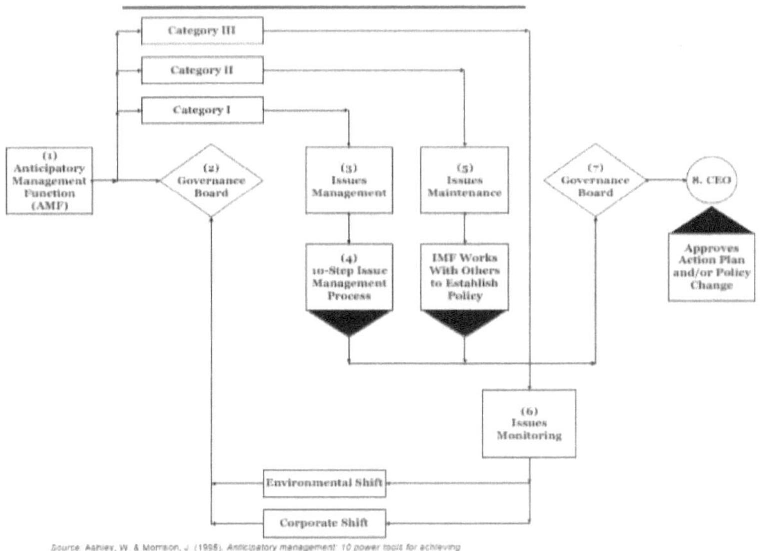

Source: Ashley, W. & Morrison, J. (1995). Anticipatory management: 10 power tools for achieving excellence into the 21st century. Leesburg, VA: Issue Action Publishing.

Responsibility for resolving the issue must rest at the senior management level. The 10-step issues management model an organization needs to implement is outlined below:

1. Issue owner appointed;
2. Issue action team;
3. Situational assessment;
4. Study results;
5. Stakeholder analysis;
6. Organizational position;
7. Stakeholder objectives;
8. Organizational objectives;
9. Action plan implementation; and
10. Measurement and fine-tuning

The steering committee, selected by the CEO reviews the action plans, including details of what is to be done, when it is to be done, why it is to be done, how much it will cost and where the money will come from.[333] The success of developing any futuring framework is not the successful integration of the anticipation system but its capacity to sustain the process of implementing it.

The next chapter will cover ways to ensure that there is sustainability and continuity of the anticipation framework.

Take Away Messages (Chapters 31-36)

- Futuring involves a structured process that has to be driven by a strategic leader's team;
- The process to determine possible external pressures that an organization may be faced is the AMP;
- AMP will not only generate useful information about the possible challenges from the external environment but assist in prioritizing the issues that would arise from the process

---

333 Ashley & Morrison, *Anticipatory*, 154.

Futuring Changing of the Guard

An organization's best-laid plans can collapse like a house of cards when key fundamentals are not deeply rooted in its culture. Planning for a successful change of leadership through mentorship tops the list.

The sharing and transfer of knowledge to build an institutional memory to benefit successive new talents are next. Just as important is a learning culture that not only focuses on training programs,

A mentally that does not compromise on quality and continuously practices strategic thinking are two others in the list. These will ensure the completeness of its future-centered orientation and that its development and leadership change are sustainable and run smoothly.

They help ensure programs and actions that increase follower engagement are sustainable when there is a passing of the baton in leadership.

Mentoring the next generation of leaders

In today's highly competitive search for leadership talent, a change in the top hierarchy without hiccups is critical for the economic sustainability and growth of an organization. It hinges on a system that subscribes to mentoring the next generation of leaders. This guarantees that what are in place to continue and improve plans for the future do not die with the exit of the incumbent leadership.

The future performance of any organization is dependent on the "thoroughness and vigor" of today's succession management or planning.[334] This is not simply a one-for-one replacement exercise and involves more than producing candidates who are copies of their predecessors. Investors of any organization would also be interested to evaluate the quality of the next generation of management talent and their level of preparedness to propel the enterprise to new heights.[335]

Succession plans, therefore, must link leadership recruitment, preparation, selection, assignment, induction and on-going development in a coherent future-oriented way.[336] There must be continuous engagement with the development of leadership candidates in the organization.[337] This is where the mentoring rubber meets the road.[338]

---

334 Seymour, S., "Boost your business value with succession planning." *Human Resource Management International Digest*, 16(2008): 3-5. doi: 10.1108/09670730810878385, p.5.

335 Seymour, *Succession*, 5

336 Fink, D., & Brayman, C., "Principals' succession and educational change." *Journal of Educational Administration*, 42(2004): 431-449. doi: 10.1108/09578230410544053.

337 Haynes, R. K., *Mentoring and Succession Management : An Evaluative Approach to the Strategic Collaboration Model.* (1991).

338 Haynes, *Mentoring.*

Roadmap for Next-Generation Leaders

Who Should Participate in Mentoring?

Succession planning should not only occur at the top of the food chain. Instead its tentacles must spread across an organization that zooms in also on those who occupy strategic and critical seats and upper management.[339] Starting from the top of the hierarchy, the board of directors must be active in all aspects of succession planning, from making decisions objectively and conducting this process with transparency.[340] While the board of directors play an active role in giving inputs, the CEO takes on the task of executing management succession.[341] He makes the ultimate decisions. As is its nature, the human resources department must also take

---

339 Conlon R. and Smith R.V. "The role of the board and the CEO in ensuring business continuity (senior manager succession management)." *Financial Executive (USA)*, 26(2010) No. 9: 52.

340 Conlon & Smith, *Continuity*, 54.

341 Conlon & Smith, *Continuity*, 54.

an active part in co-designing the process, managing the infrastructure[342] and facilitating everything.[343]

Mentoring and Action-Based Learning

Most human development professionals subscribe to the axiom that seventy percent of career development takes place on the job.[344] Hewitt (2009) quotes Athey (2004) in stating that the traditional linear process of talent development needs to be replaced with a model of "develop, deploy and connect" to manage succession planning positively to ensure a positive outcome. The sharp focus of action-oriented developmental activities is also a hallmark of an exemplary succession planning system.[345] This entails mentors interacting with candidates in real life action-learning programs to hone their leadership skills [346] and helping in their career development.[347] Such schemes involve exposing the candidates to several functional and product areas.[348]

Mentoring could also involve issuing rotating assignments that cuts across disciplines, divisions and geographical

---

342 Industries, H., "Who's next in line?" *Business,* 20(2004): 30-32. doi: 10.1108/02580540410533262, 31.

343 Conlon & Smith, *Continuity,* 54.

344 Fulmer, R.M., Stumpf, S.A., Bleak, J., "The strategic development of high potential leaders." *Strategy and Leadership,* 37(2009) 3:17-22.

345 Groves, K. S., "Integrating leadership development and succession planning best practices." *Journal of Management Development,* 26(2007): 239-260. doi: 10.1108/02621710710732146, 249.

346 Hewitt, S. D., "The secrets of successful succession planning in the new age wave." *Industrial and Commercial Training,* 41(2009): 181-186. doi: 10.1108/00197850910962751.

347 Groves, *Integrating,* 244.

348 Groves, *Integrating,* 250.

locations.[349] Action-based learning brings real world business problems or change projects into an interactive and simulated environment where candidates are challenged to solve these problems.[350] For example, they could even take on a project to turn around an unprofitable department.[351]

An important ingredient in the relationship between mentors and mentees is the discussion on challenges the potential leaders face.[352] They are able to then express their goals, describing what is important and defining what success means to them.[353] Such interactions have the added benefit of roughening out the edges in a candidate's managerial and administrative competence[354] and encourage him to also make decisions through critical thinking.[355] This broadening of education through action-based learning and assignments creates a workforce who are more adaptable to moving and working across various departments with ease.[356] The

---

349 Fulmer et al., *Strategic*, 19.

350 Industries, *Next*, 31.

351 Xavier, S., "Developing emerging leaders: a new solution to an old problem." *Business Strategy Series*, 8(2007): 343-349. doi: 10.1108/17515630710684457. p.345.

352 Lipscomb, C. E., Martin, E. R., & Peay, W. J., "Building the Next Generation of Leaders: The NLM/AAHSL Leadership Fellows Program." *Journal of Library Administration*, 49(2009): 847-867. doi: 10.1080/01930820903396970.

353 Lipscomb, Martin, & Peay, *Generation*.

354 Van Amburgh, J., Surratt, C. K., Green, J. S., Gallucci, R. M., Colbert, J., Zatopek, S. L., et al., "Succession planning in US pharmacy schools." *American Journal of Pharmaceutical Education*, 74(2010). Retrieved from http://www.pubmedcentral.nih.gov/articlerender. fcgi?artid=2907851&tool=pmcentrez&rendertype=abstract.

355 Guinn, S.L., "Succession planning without job titles," *Career Development International*, 5(2000): 390-393. p.391.

356 Hewitt, *Succession*.

candidates' involvement in project teams also opens up opportunities for them to demonstrate their capabilities outside of their comfort zones.[357]

The executive team and board members are responsible for designing these action-learning projects and their respective topics they are meant to teach.[358] The candidates learn from such in-depth exposure because this what is expected of them as managers.[359] Senior executives and managers must also offer support, where necessary, and monitor the progress of the candidates.[360] This involves continuous re-assessment of their core strengths, suggestions on areas they need to improve on and their leadership qualities that need attention.

Awareness of Future Needs

The formation of candidates must correspond with what is required from a leader of tomorrow.[361] It must also consider key technological, economic and social trends that will influence how businesses are conducted and challenge employees.[362] This strategy of thinking ahead is an investment

---

357 Clutterbuck, D., & Cox, T., "Mentoring by wire." *Training Journal,* (2005): 35-39. Retrieved from http://search.proquest.com/ docview/ 202952384?accountid= 13479, p.12.

358 Groves, *Integrating.*

359 Groves, *Integrating.*

360 Groves, *Integrating*; Fulmer et al., *Strategic,* 19

361 Fulmer et al., *Strategic.*

362 Hills,A.,"Successionplanning—orsmarttalentmanagement?"*Industrialand Commercial Training,* 41(2009): 3-8. doi: 10.1108/00197850910927697.

on an effective passing of the baton that places the next generation of leaders in a position to tackle the challenges they will face.[363]

---

363 Hammett, P., "The paradox of gifted leadership: developing the generation of leaders." *Industrial and Commercial Training*, 40(2008): 3-9. doi: 10.1108/00197850810841585. p.8.

Stewards of Knowledge and Craft

One view of organizational learning is that it springs from social interaction among employees who share a common interest in an area of work and master it with practice.[364] For this to take place like-minded members of a group or community must be proficient in the knowledge and skill of their particular work.[365] This concept is called Communities of Practice (CoP) and a way of promoting the exchange of specific information internally through action-based learning. The ability to embed this in an organization will help a leader to sustain a change culture because CoPs can develop and preserve long-term organizational or institutional memory[366].

364 Higgins, D., & Aspinall, C., "Learning to learn: a case for developing small firm owner/managers." *Journal of Small Business and Enterprise Development*, 18(2011): 43-57. doi:10.1108/14626001111106424, p.45.
365 Higgins and Aspinall, *Learning*, 45.
366 Retna and Ng, *Communities*, 44.

As CoP consists of a group of individuals pursuing a deeper understanding of their expertise, [367] what they have been able to mine is a property of relationships – the networks of human interaction that create and transform it.[368] These members are, therefore the stewards of knowledge as a result of their common passion, the fruit of which is an improved practice of their craft.[369,370] Their interaction promotes learning through knowledge transfer.

As mentioned in Iaquinto, et al. (2011), in order to have a successful CoP, it is necessary that:

- They gain the support of leadership who act as sponsors;
- Members demonstrate a sense of ownership of the CoP topic;
- Members are willing to participate and communicate in meetings and sharing of their expertise in a specific area;
- Members are willing to identify gaps in their knowledge and attempt to fill them;
- They ensure that the focus of the CoP reflects the organization's core business;
- They clarify the value of CoP participation and communicating the benefits clearly at an individual and organizational levels; and
- They avoid having one coordinator throughout the life of the CoP but embrace a successful method of transfer of coordination.

---

367 Retna and Ng, *Communities*, 41.
368 Retna and Ng, *Communities*, 42.
369 Retna and Ng, *Communities*, 43.
370 Retna and Ng, *Communities*, 43.

The Change Buy-in

It is noteworthy that the formation of training programs in organizations in a large majority of firms do not significantly correlate with the existence of a learning culture.[371] In many instances, it seems training sessions are not enough to encourage learning among their members because their goal is only to develop human resources.[372] West (1994) states that the concept of learning encompasses more than implementing a high degree of training for employees. Grinsven and Visser (2011) notes that the effect of knowledge conversion is especially strong in first order learning, where it is action-oriented, routine, incremental and exists within certain norms and assumptions. The effect from the second order is weak.[373] This means that formalized training does not entail learning by changing the mental models, norms and

---

371 Rebelo and Gomes, *Conditioning*, 187.

372 Rebelo and Gomes, *Conditioning*, 187.

373 Grinsven, M. V., & Visser, M., "Empowerment, knowledge conversion and dimensions of organizational learning." *The Learning Organization*, 18(2011): 378-391. doi:10.1108/09696471111151729. p.385.

assumptions that underpin day-to-day actions and routines.[374] It also does not prepare an organization adequately to deal with turbulence, and complex and dynamic changes with the second order of learning.[375]

Experiential change programs (ECPs) are useful during change, and the affective outcomes from its stakeholders active learning[376] can have a positive influence in a company.[377] In ECPs, the participants or stakeholders engage emotionally, and viscerally through simulations, games and other experience-based methods.[378] This high level of interactivity encourages the study of new procedures and test those involved in safe environments while they attempt to perfect fresh methods.[379] This is in contrast to the traditional way of considering new ideas such as memos, presentations and meetings where the visceral engagement is absent.[380]

ECP, on the other hand, decreases and even eliminates stakeholders' resistance to changes. They are motivated and committed to implement them.[381] Its buy-in effectiveness is chiefly due to greater organizational learning.[382] As the nature and intensity of the stakeholders' feelings are evoked during

---

374 Grinsven and Visser, *Empowerment*, 380.
375 Grinsven and Visser, *Empowerment*, 380.
376 Russ, T. L., "An exploratory study of an experiential change program's impact on participants' affective outcomes." *Leadership & Organization Development Journal*, 32(2011): 493-509. doi:10.1108/01437731111146587, p.493.
377 Russ, *Experiential*, 494.
378 Russ, *Experiential*, 494.
379 Russ, *Experiential*, 494.
380 Russ, *Experiential*, 495.
381 Russ, *Experiential*, 495.
382 Russ, *Experiential*, 495.

ECPs the result is a long-term sustainable change.[383] This outcome is further entrenched because there is alignment between managers and leaders,[384] which is a motivating factor for their followers to rally behind them.[385]

---

383 Russ, *Experiential*, 495.
384 Russ, *Experiential*, 503.
385 Russ, *Experiential*, 504.

Quality: The Sustainable Drive

When quality is maintained it helps the rank and file to focus on continuous change. But keeping this up is a challenge for every leader.[386] The solution to sustain quality, therefore, is to continuously improve it.[387] Leaders can make sure of this through active review, enhancement and maintenance in all aspects of an organization's performance.[388]

This can be done with a framework such as TQM or Total Quality Management. Using this, an organization can incorporate active review assessments and map out plans to improve operations and outcomes.[389] The first step is for leaders and followers to agree on objectives, and then to constantly identify and prioritize the most important items to act on, based on existing state of affairs.[390] The focus

---

386 Smith, I., "Organisational quality and organisational change: Interconnecting paths to effectiveness." *Library Management*, 32(2011): 111-128. doi:10.1108/01435121111102629, p.112.
387 Smith, *Change*, 113.
388 Smith, *Change*, 113.
389 Smith, *Change*, 119.
390 Smith, *Change*, 120.

on quality and change, and understanding how both are interconnected is a proactive approach to managing them.[391] All of this drives to make the organization's change initiatives more sustainable.

---

391 Smith, *Change*, 127.

The Future Scorecard Strategy

According to Amsteus (2008), foresight has been defined in a way to make it and thus strategic thinking measurable.[392] It is then possible to investigate empirically and quantitatively the degree of the existence of strategic thinking.[393] He defines foresight as:

Degree of analyzing present contingencies and degree of moving the analysis of present contingencies across time, and degree of analyzing a desired future or states a degree ahead in time with regard to contingencies under control, as well as degree of analyzing courses of action a degree ahead in time to arrive at the desired future state.

The definition is founded on the three dimensions of actions. The first analyzes conditions that form the base to identify objectives to achieve and how to obtain them. The second is

---

392 Amsteus, M., "Managerial foresight: concept and measurement." *Foresight*, 10(2008): 53-66. doi:10.1108/14636680810856026, p.53.
393 Amsteus, *Foresight*, 53.

the desired future state and third are contingencies under the control of an individual (e.g., Manager). The present state or condition represents why something is done or "a matter of the resolution on the measurement scale between the past and the future."[394]

Balanced Scorecard

Dereli (2007) discusses the balanced scorecard as a tool to measure and assess the effectiveness of strategic thinking or foresight in the public sector. The tool was introduced because financial measures alone were not adequate to assess the extent of strategic thinking.[395] For it to be effective it also needs to consider other measures that an organization's vision and strategy produce as well.[396]

In describing the scorecard, Thomas (2007) examines what US business schools need to do in light of the increased competition they face from Europe, Asia and Latin America. He said it provides a disciplined framework for monitoring, evaluating and controlling the evolutionary path of the business schools' strategy and positioning. The scorecard has elements that are critical to setting goals, business planning, capital allocations, strategic initiatives and feedback. It also has learning frameworks that ease strategic thinking.[397]

---

394 Amsteus, *Foresight*, 58.
395 Dereli, C., "The developing environment for strategy formation in the smaller local authority." *International Journal of Public Sector Management*, 20(2007): 366-379. doi:10.1108/09513550710772495
396 Dereli, *Strategy*, 3.
397 Thomas, H., "Business school strategy and the metrics for success." *Journal of Management Development*, 26(2007): 33-42. doi:10.1108/02621710710720068, p.40.

Another feature of the tool is that it links strategy to key performance indicators (KPIs).

In using the scorecard, key managers are able to detect gaps and weaknesses and allocate resources to correct them, before setting priorities for the long term as strategies emerge in any dynamic environment.[398]

Future scorecard

This is a continuous measurement tool organizations employ to assess strategies that have been implemented. As it is designed to monitor future developments new solutions are constantly introduced to address them, over and above what are already in place.[399] This scorecard assists organizations to develop internal scenarios to complement external ones in order to provide strategic foresight.[400] In addition, it monitors critical market indicators and internal performance indexes that are not considered in existing strategies.[401]

The future scorecard was developed based on a creative learning culture and experiences in the fields of future thinking and strategic management.[402] It enlarges perspectives and the integrated non-financial and external indicators, compared to the balanced scorecard that focuses only on currently followed strategies.[403]

---

398 Thomas, *Metrics*, 40.

399 Fink, A., Marr, B., Siebe, A., & Kuhle, J.-P., "The future scorecard: combining external and internal scenarios to create strategic foresight." *Management Decision*, 43(2005): 360-381. doi:10.1108/00251740510589751, p.378.

400 Fink, Marr, Siebe, & Kuhle, *Scorecard*, 379.

401 Fink, Marr, Siebe, & Kuhle, *Scorecard*, 378.

402 Fink, Marr, Siebe, & Kuhle, *Scorecard*, 379.

403 Fink, Marr, Siebe, & Kuhle, *Scorecard*, 378.

Comprehensive Performance Assessment (CPA)

Dereli (2007) discusses the use of comprehensive performance assessment (CPA) as a method for the public sector to assess how a local government implements strategy. Just like the balanced scorecard, CPA has a structural model that incorporates vision and strategy. It also has the ability to evaluate and understand on how strategic management is measured in the public sector. CPA focuses on the effectiveness of delivery of strategy and vision.[404]

Take Away Messages (Chapters 37-42)

- The success of the futuring process can be measured;
- Leaders need to understand the various measures that can be implemented to ensure that the futuring process is sustainable.

---

404 Dereli, *Strategy*, 375.

Part 05

THE CULTURE GLUE

Elemental Force
of Culture

Today, of the one hundred companies that existed in the 1900s, only sixteen are still in existence.[405] Only twenty-nine companies in Fortune magazine's first list of the Top 500 largest companies in 1965 are still included today while 46 percent of those companies listed a decade ago have dropped off the rival Forbes 500 list.[406] This highlights the need for organizations to undergo constant change in order to remain at the top of their league.

As mentioned at the beginning of the book, changes are unpredictable and are often dramatic. This implies that no organization can remain the same for long and survive without undergoing change.[407] One of the fundamental conversions an organization has to manage is its culture;

---

405 Cameron, K.S., & Quinn, R.E., *Diagnosing and changing organizational culture: Based on the competing values framework (3rd ed.).* (San Francisco: Jossey-Bass, 2006). (ISBN: 9780470650264).
406 Cameron & Quinn, *Diagnosing*, 9.
407 Cameron & Quinn, *Diagnosing*, 10.

without which there is little hope of enduring improvement in performance.[408] Without a focus on this, leaders and their employees will find it difficult to find alignment because there is no glue that sticks them together and a learning organization also cannot operate effectively. Finally, without the focus on culture, an organization has a bleak chance of maintaining any sustainable change.

To ensure permanence in any cultural conversion, the fundamental goals, values and expectations of organizations and individuals need to alter. Otherwise, cultural change would be superficial and of short duration.[409] Eighty-two percent of executives agreed that corporate culture affects the long-term financial performance of companies.[410] Yet, research shows that sixty-two percent of executives surveyed did not monitor the state of corporate culture at all.[411] In this last chapter, we highlight the importance of constantly working to develop and manage the culture of an organization in any transition mentioned earlier in the book. These occurrences include altering an organization's structure and decentralization of its decision making, the introduction of an anticipatory process or even the simple alignment between leadership and the rank and file. Culture serves as the elemental force and glue that ensure the sustainability of any of change.

---

408 Cameron & Quinn, *Diagnosing*, 12.
409 Cameron & Quinn, *Diagnosing*, 13.
410 Wahl, A., "Stop the Rot." *Canadian Business*, 78(2005): 119-120. p.119.
411 Wahl, *Stop*, 119.

The Aligning Cohesive Force

Cultural change is the interplay between individual growth and organizational development.[412] Individuals create organizations that in turn are a collection of people and changing them should be the first step in any process that seeks to prepare it for any transformation.[413] Branson (2008) mentions that too much emphasis has often been placed upon making conversions that influence the external dimensions of an organization and too little has been placed upon making essential ones that influence those that are internal.[414]

Culture allows organizations to align all of its external and internal efforts in order to meet its needs in the midst of change.[415]

---

412 McGuire, J. B., Rhodes, G., & Palus, C. J., "Inside out: Transforming your leadership culture." *Leadership in Action*, 27(2008): 3–7. doi:10.1002/lia.1226.

413 Branson, C. M., "Achieving organisational change through values alignment." *Journal of Educational Administration*, 46(2008): 376–395. doi:10.1108/09578230810869293, p.392.

414 Branson, *Organizational*, 377.

415 Branson, *Organizational*, 380.

The influence of culture becomes evident when people come together to satisfy needs and wants, and to clarify how to accomplish things.[416] It has a profound influence on everyone's behavior as it serves to draw all members together to create a sense of cohesion, which then acts as an informal control mechanism that helps to define acceptable behavior.[417] Culture provides employees with information that is necessary for them to function and guide employees to know how they can support the company's mission.[418]

When leaders examine beliefs and thinking, they increase awareness of how and why they make decisions.[419] They gain new insights into what is working and what is not.[420] Leaders and followers can then begin consciously to build a bridge between the hidden, internal drivers and the visible, external actions.[421] Building alignment is about enhancing the group's capacity to think and act in new synergistic ways, with full coordination and a sense of unity, because each person knows the hearts and minds of others.[422]

Values guide our decision and behavior choices because of how we perceive the world. Those we select in turn affect our actions.[423] Values also determine the selection and

---

416 Branson, *Organizational*, 380.

417 Branson, *Organizational*, 380.

418 Branson, *Organizational*, 380.

419 McGuire, Rhodes, & Palus, *Transforming*, 5.

420 McGuire, Rhodes, & Palus, *Transforming*, 5.

421 McGuire, Rhodes, & Palus, *Transforming*, 6.

422 Branson, *Organizational*, 383.

423 Fitzpatrick, R. L., "A literature review exploring values alignment as a proactive approach to conflict management." *International Journal of Conflict Management*, 18(2007): 280–305. doi:10.1108/1044406071082600 7. p.290.

perception of external stimulus. A person's cognitive-affective appraisal of a situation in relation to both "means" and "ends" affects decision-making and behavioral choices.[424] The implementation of comprehensive values alignment process will allow an organization to prepare an individual's psyche to cope constructively with changes to ensure its long-term viability and success.[425] Individuals are able to make decisions on external stimuli by giving a values-based response.[426] The organization, as a result, becomes more efficient and effective in its decisions. The end goal of focusing on developing the culture of an organization is for leaders not to focus on shorter-term micro issues but instead be free to focus on longer-term strategic macro decisions.

Cultural knowledge is the collective shared information that accompanies the behaviors and practices of people. This includes commonly held beliefs about an organization's purpose, structure, strategy, members, task accomplishment, adaptation and change, relations among people, and individual learning mechanisms.[427]

Corporate culture is not about health benefits or subsidized cafeteria. It is about the attitudes inherent in how to run a business and the expectations that are communicated explicitly and implicitly to employees.[428] Culture sets the norms

---

424 Fitzpatrick, *Values*, 290.

425 Branson, *Organizational*, 392.

426 Fitzpatrick, *Values*, 282.

427 Lyon, A., "Participants' use of cultural knowledge as cultural capital in a dot-com start-up organization." *Management Communication Quarterly*, 18(2004): 175-203.

428 Wahl, *Stop*, 120.

on everything, but it is often undetectable.[429] It manifests as the implicit assumptions that define the human condition and its relationship with the environment. These assumptions emerge as contracts and norms. Rules, procedures and policies emerge from these beliefs, which govern human interaction. Culture enables an organization to manage successful performance, about how to coordinate work and how to reward employees.

In contrast, artefacts are visible. They are represented by buildings in which we work, sizes and shapes of offices, arrangements of visions statements, formal goals, logos, themes, power structures, communication structures, and forms of recognition in use. Changing culture involves addressing each of these various levels.[430] It would seem wise to focus initially on the alignment of values of a desired culture by altering the artefacts simply because it effects a cultural change easiest. However, the gains from such efforts can be short lived and passing judgment on culture based on artefacts alone is unwise.[431] This is because these are surface things that lead only to a superficial understanding of an organization when it could be driven by a different system of values compared to similar groups.[432]

---

429 McGuire, Rhodes, & Palus, *Transforming*, 4.
430 Cameron & Quinn, *Diagnosing*, 20.
431 Thornbury, J., "Creating a living culture: the challenges for business leaders." *Corporate Governance*, 3(2003): 68–79. doi:10.1108/14720700310474073.
432 Thornbury, *Culture*, 71.

Core Value Imperative

How people act is harder to change and the benefits last longer.[433] The most obvious manifestation of culture is the implicit behavior of its members. It involves the way in which people interact, and the extent to which innovative or activity is tolerated and encouraged. Often this is described as "just the way things are done around here." Culture is the collective action of employees, which, ideally, mirrors the values in which the company's leaders believe.[434] It is simply a human system of closely held beliefs that require certain behaviors and exclude others.[435]

These are useful as a differentiation strategy especially when a company's marketplace is becoming increasingly commoditized.[436] Where they are negative in a customer's opinion, an organization could lose business if its customers

---

433 Thornbury, *Culture*, 72.

434 Wahl, *Stop*, 120.

435 McGuire, Rhodes, & Palus, *Transforming*, 4.

436 Bacon, T. R., "Driving cultural change through behavioral differentiation at Westinghouse." *Business Strategy Series*, 8(2007):350–357. doi:10.1108/17515630710684466.

had viable alternatives. Conversely, when behaviors are more positively viewed, it could gain customers in situations where other competitive factors are relatively equal. They can have an attractive effect (positive differentiation) or a repulsive effect (negative differentiation) and organizations have the power to use them to manage their competitiveness as part of the strategy.[437] Fundamental to all this is the fact that the values used to guide these changes are to be shared by, believed in and meaningful to people throughout the organization.[438]

Core Values

These are the timeless guiding principles for behavior, decisions and actions. They are the fundamental ideals that an organization will never give up.[439] Core values are taken-for-granted beliefs at the heart of a culture and they drive behavior.[440] Values reflect basic issues or problems that societies address to regulate human actions.[441] Their patterns are suggestive of various coherent societal solutions to human regulation problems. They develop through the influences of culture, society and personality and exist in highly organized networks such as that of an organization.[442]

---

437 Bacon, *Cultural*, 351.
438 Thornbury, *Culture*, 72.
439 Thornbury, *Culture*, 71.
440 McGuire, Rhodes, & Palus, *Transforming*, 5.
441 Klenke, K., "Corporate values as multi-level, multi-domain antecedents of leader behaviors." *International Journal of Manpower*, 26(2005): 50–66. doi:10.1108/01437720510587271.
442 Klenke, *Values*, 52.

Values serve as strong regulatory guides by specifying modes of behavior that are socially acceptable.[443] Decisions are the go-betweens, interpreting inbound data and translating cultural beliefs into action. Core beliefs are so strong that they drive decisions in subtle and automatic ways, and often decision makers are not even aware of them. Culture produces a belief-based decision engine that creates a form of assurance.[444] Core values become second nature over time and acted upon without thought.[445]

While a few companies have statement of values that reflect accurately what is at the heart of their culture, for many others core values remain unconscious and difficult to articulate or identify.[446] This is because they are deeply engrained and unconscious, and, therefore, very slow and difficult to change. A great deal of patience is required to convert these into visible behavior.[447] One can conceptualize corporate values, however, into three subsets: work, leadership and spiritual that operate at the individual, organizational and global levels, respectively.[448]

Values can serve as a unifying force, providing that both corporate and individuals are reasonably congruent as they bind people together as they move toward achieving company goals.[449] Conversely, conflicting vales are generators of stress

---

443 Klenke, *Values*, 52.
444 McGuire, Rhodes, & Palus, *Transforming*, 5.
445 Thornbury, *Culture*, 71.
446 Thornbury, *Culture*, 71.
447 Thornbury, *Culture*, 72.
448 Klenke, *Values*, 52.
449 Klenke, *Values*, 51.

and friction that undermine managerial leadership, and therefore need clear and consistent principles that permeate and define the organization.[450] Values can provide coherence and a sense of purpose to an individual's behavior that conforms to the needs of an organization.[451] For a company to have a successful change initiative, there must be cultural beliefs to drive decisions that create the needed changes in actions to imbue an organization.[452]

---

450 Klenke, *Values*, 51.
451 Klenke, *Values*, 52.
452 McGuire, Rhodes, & Palus, *Transforming*, 5.

Relationships in Context

Edward Hall (1959) describes culture as an unseen but powerful force that holds everyone captive. Culture hides more than is revealed.[453] Hall is famous for his Context Theory and Time Theory.

Context Theory

The meanings that people exchange in ways other than language are usually referred to as context.[454] In a high-context culture, communication involves a more indirect or implicit style where people tend to rely on body language, intonations of speech and hidden meanings. Friendship and extensive family networks exist in high-context cultures.[455] Written agreements in such situations are not necessarily binding but oral agreements are.[456]

---

453 Hall, E. T., *The silent language*. (New York: Doubleday, 1959): 53.
454 Pan, W., "Thinking culturally : A study of culture and politeness." *US-China Foreign Language,* 6(2008): 36–40, p.37.
455 Luan, M., "Comparison of the Studies on Intercultural Communication." *US-China Foreign Language,* 10(2012): 1207-1213, p.1208.
456 Luan, *Interculturally*, 1208.

Low-context cultures dislike ambiguity and prefer clarity established through clear information and detailed communication, which is through language.[457] These environmentstendtocompartmentalizepersonalrelationships, work, and aspects of their personal life.[458] Communication is also more formal and explicit.[459] Politeness clashes over the verbal, and non-verbal, and acceptable rituals between cultures can easily take place because communicators tend to find meanings in words when they interact with their high-context counterparts.[460]

Time Theory

In monochronic or sequential cultures, time is tangible and they equate this to money. Life is controlled through schedules and appointments, and the preference is to work in private offices without interruptions.[461] They frown upon spare or waiting time. In synchronic or polychronic cultures, the emphasis is on human relationships rather than schedules or deadlines. Punctuality is less important. Maintenance of harmonious relations is considered most important.[462] Hall perceives that different cultural attitudes towards aspects such as time could create frustration, irritation and even hostility in international communication.[463]

---

457 Luan, *Interculturally*, 1208.
458 Luan, *Interculturally*, 1209.
459 Luan, *Interculturally*, 1209.
460 Pan, *Culturally*, p.37.
461 Luan, *Interculturally*, 1209.
462 Luan, *Interculturally*, 1209.
463 Luan, *Interculturally*, 1209.

Kraus (2008) illustrates this by describing the cultural difference that exists in Germany and China. China is described as a high-context culture where interpersonal relationships are intensive and communication is mostly implicit. Agreements and contracts are formed verbally and the feeling for time is polychromic.[464] In contrast, Germany's interpersonal relationships are rather transient and loose, where communication is very explicit and preference is strictly written agreements. The feeling of time is monochromic.[465] Thus, in the German culture, a company is efficient when it uses its available resources in a way that it reaches the optimal maximal output. Personal relationships, conflicts, harmony, and group coherence are only factors in relation to the company's results. This contrasts with the Chinese culture where they view output as a function of optimal input. Interpersonal factors are regarded to have the highest possible importance for the achievement of company's goals.[466]

---

464 Kraus, S., Mitter, C., & Siems, F., "Doing business in China: a German perspective on joint business ventures." *International Journal of Business Research*, 8(2008): 99+, p.101.
465 Kraus, *Business*, 101.
466 Kraus, *Business*, 103.

Hidden Drivers

When leaders are asked to look at change initiatives, they are really asking followers and individuals to alter their beliefs in some way.[467] Leaders are expected to move beyond external change and move towards an internal transformation in culture beyond that of their operational plans. When an organization unearths and examine beliefs, values, and assumptions intentionally, it draws out the hidden or unconscious drivers for what is happening or not happening. By examining the internal dimensions, leaders introduce the possibility of new thinking and beliefs and therefore fresh decisions and behaviors. They achieve this by participating together in the culture change process to enlarge the mental and emotional space for transformation. This allows them to make unexpected and innovative decisions, allowing an inside-out approach to change.[468]

Leadership must play the role of designer, teacher, and be stewards of a shared vision while also being able to challenge

---

467 McGuire, Rhodes, & Palus, *Transforming*, 3.
468 McGuire, Rhodes, & Palus, *Transforming*, 3.

prevailing mental models of their followers. They should also be learning leaders who are responsible for building an organization where the staff are expanding and enhancing their capabilities continuously to share their future. Leaders need to ensure the organization's vision transmits firm, explicit values that shape the culture and subsequently actions.[469] They have to ensure these values are derived through a process of inclusiveness and involvement with employees.[470]

---

469 Baines, *Knowledge*, 204.
470 Baines, *Knowledge*, 204.

Alignment of Values

The values of individuals and the organization must align in order for a business to remain competitive and excel in today's challenging economic climate. This alignment streamlines operations as it improves the capacity to make effective decisions. Aspects of culture, including its related components such as values and behavioral are areas that need great attention in any culture evaluation and change management process. It does not only involve the participation of leaders but also engage all individuals. Working on values means placing emphasis on people first and working on change from the inside out.

Organizations are essentially cultures of relationships where value priorities are what glue people together.[471] There needs to be sufficient common of these to sustain the ties.[472] An organization's strategy runs counter to the belief about "how

---

471 Hall, B. P., "Values development and learning organizations." *Journal of Knowledge Management*, 5(2001): 19–32. doi:10.1108/ 13673270110384374.
472 Hall, *Values*, 21.

things are done around here".[473] Individuals come with their own set of values and when they form a group or organization, it does not possess a set of values unless a majority personally and authentically embrace common values within a proposed set.[474] Their respective values are automatic but are most often subliminal driving influences in determining their behavior.[475] In the context of group values, these are only guiding concepts, as they still require people to choose to act in alignment with them.[476] Each person could falsely claim to support such nominated values if these are to their advantage to do so.[477] Some behaviors may seem to be aligned to an organization's values but in actuality are only to their own personal values. Where individuals do not embrace collective values, an organization cannot implement them.[478]

Employees or followers have an affective commitment because they have an emotional attachment to, identification with and positive involvement in the organization.[479] Because of this commitment, there is a need to nurture an accommodating consciousness within each employee by cultivating an alignment between their values with those that underpin the success of the organization.[480] Values are visible threads and where there is alignment between an organization and individual there is a natural connection among people in

---

473 McGuire, Rhodes, & Palus, *Transforming*, 5.
474 Branson, *Organizational*.
475 Branson, *Organizational*, 382.
476 Branson, *Organizational*, 381.
477 Branson, *Organizational*, 382.
478 Branson, *Organizational*, 382.
479 Branson, *Organizational*, 380.
480 Branson, *Organizational*, 380.

the company. That relationship extends externally and could also include customers.[481]

When it is unaligned, an organization struggles to maintain its identity during periods of change as its people operate by objectives and obligations rather than by preference because there is little or no awareness of the values that underpin strategies. Often, people also hold allegiance to a plurality of partially incompatible beliefs and values based on assumptions they hold about their own entitlements, constraints, and preferred courses of action.[482]

Leaders need to ensure there are well-articulated values instilled in its people and upheld in behaviors across all levels in order to strengthen and improve those principles.[483] People must support the desired values that will become the norm through behavioral changes and personal development activities.[484] Organizations expect employees to reflect their beliefs. When they are unaligned it is an indication there is conflict between what employees consider important and what is stated policy.[485] But when they are in harmony, what exists is a dynamic ongoing process where leaders need to define values clearly, and examine, prioritize, and translate them into specific behavioral terms.[486]

---

481 Branson, *Organizational*, 381.
482 Branson, *Organizational*, 381.
483 Thornbury, *Culture*, 77.
484 Thornbury, *Culture*, 72.
485 Fitzpatrick, *Values*.
486 Fitzpatrick, *Values*, 298.

Path to Alignment

Alignment is not a naturally occurring process since values have a subjective dimension.[487] Branson (2008) suggests that an organization must first discern and clarify what are essential to characterize the company so it can achieve its vision and purpose.[488] The second step is bringing about alignment where each person is encouraged to support these values in their work each day.[489]

Values of the Organization

These appear as adjunct rather than integral and are an embedded component of culture. It is likely, then, that any preferred values are likely to remain vague and abstract to an employee.[490] What must therefore be done is to positively influence employees to help them understand and support the place and significance of these values with the company's culture.[491]

---

487 Branson, *Organizational*, 381.
488 Branson, *Organizational*, 382.
489 Branson, *Organizational*, 382.
490 Branson, *Organizational*, 383.
491 Branson, *Organizational*, 383.

The key to doing this is to help employees understand how the organization's values are formed and implemented in order to create an appropriate and successful culture.[492] They need to know factors that form any preferred strategic values so that they clearly see how they are important to an organization's culture and how they can lead to a more successful outfit.[493] Only then can employees align their personal values with those perceived as strategic to an organization.[494]

Core Mission

The initial work to align what are important to employees with those of a company should include the formation of the core mission. This will help them to understand the significance of their company values, so they will be in a better position to support and adopt the core mission.[495] This will give the company the ability to identify the crucial ingredients that enable the rank and file to develop confidence in its ability to achieve its goals by either reinforcing its group and individual strengths or overcoming its weaknesses through targeted professional development. Ultimately, the organization will be able to affirm the existing talent and their worth in the group, and confirm its commitment to employees. The organization's values and why they are prized will subsequently become apparent.[496]

---

492 Branson, *Organizational*, 383.
493 Branson, *Organizational*, 384.
494 Branson, *Organizational*, 384.
495 Branson, *Organizational*, 385.
496 Branson, *Organizational*, 385.

Avoid overloading

One must note the focus should only be on a limited number of values because an overload will be too difficult for employees to support each one equally.[497] These values must also be converted into guiding beliefs for clarity so that they will produce a positive outcome for everyone.[498] When an employee authentically subscribes to every belief and value, what logically develops are positive behavioral outcomes.[499] Where organizations have predetermined what these are and reflective of the commitment to its values, each employee knows how he will be judged and assessed.[500]

This alignment process is then able to provide a discrete and valuable contribution to the individual consciousness of each employee.[501] This allows them to have an all-embracing understanding of the culture of the organization and as a result, they are able to align their personal values more easily with their employer's, which will give them a heightened sense of meaning and fulfilment in their workplace.[502]

What follows after the core mission is formed, is the listing of its indicators of success that members must be committed to. It provides the stimulus for everyone to become engaged

---

497 Branson, *Organizational*, 385.
498 Branson, *Organizational*, 385.
499 Branson, *Organizational*, 386.
500 Branson, *Organizational*, 386.
501 Branson, *Organizational*, 386.
502 Branson, *Organizational*, 386.

and provide their respective contribution to the group's activities.[503] This increases the motivation for them to develop an affective commitment and to adopt the groups' strategic values.[504]

----

503 Branson, *Organizational*, 385.
504 Branson, *Organizational*, 385.

What Works in Multi-Cultural Asia

Globalization has forced many leaders to venture into new territories and cultures. This has been evident in Asia as many entrepreneurs have invested in the region to take advantage of its booming economies. The result is a global economic environment that is undergoing transformation, which in turn has led to the reconfiguration of the work structure and labor arrangements.[505] It has constituted a need for a leader to understand the importance of intercultural communication. They must know how to improve their staff's cultural awareness and intercultural competence of the incoming expatriate hires.

Today, organizations engage in international business to acquire knowledge and skills to enhance their global

---

505 Atkins, S. G., Bolten, J., Dodd, C., Everett, A. M., Graf, A., Hill, L. B., Walters, T., "The Intercultural Communication Motivation Scale: an instrument to assess motivational training needs of candidates for international assignments." *Human Resource Management*, 48(2009): 717-744, p.718.

operations.[506] Communication and culture are closely interlinked, where a country's unique culture tends to remain unchanged at a deep level, such as values, beliefs, or attitudes.[507]

Intercultural communication now involves interaction between individuals from different religious, societal, ethnic, and educational backgrounds.[508] Ineffective communication could lead to misunderstandings because of the lack of cultural knowledge. Technology and globalization are causing the workplace to shrink and have spawned a rise in virtual teams.[509] Typically, organizations comprise of colleagues from various cultures.

The skills of communication and the need to manage people from other cultures are no longer an option. It is now a requirement for success.[510] Many leaders, when engaging across borders, must recognize cultural characteristics in a way that communication does not derail work projects.[511] The following are some suggestions for leaders to bring about alignment among various cultures in their organizations in Asia today.

A global organization encounters tremendous changes. Conflicts often arise due to differences in purposes, perceptions,

---

506 Atkins et al., *Intercultural*, 736.
507 Luan, *Interculturally*, 1207.
508 Luan, *Interculturally*, 1207.
509 Zofi, Y., "Why Cross-Cultural Communication is Critical to Virtual Teams and How to Overcome the Intercultural Disconnect." *People & Strategy*, 35(2012): 7–9, p.7.
510 Zofi, *Cross-cultural*, 7.
511 Zofi, *Cross-cultural*, 7.

personality, ambiguity and communication problems in the context of varying social and political environments.[512] Global leaders must have enough knowledge of the national and organizational norms to internalize and create a strong corporate culture that achieves social synergy.[513]

A Korean start-up, Avaro, is a good case study. It seemingly had many conditions that were conducive to a successful, working internationalization.[514] However, it still failed because it carried much of its national and cultural baggage.[515] Avaro operated in its home country and wanted to keep its Korean identity.[516] But this high level of patriotism hampered its ability to raise further investment funding from overseas non-Korean venture capital investors. It subsequently crippled its ability to realize its technological opportunities overseas.[517] The development and diffusion of innovation is not only a process of technological evolution but also requires a social adaptive process.[518]

---

512 Zorlu, K., & Hacıoğlu, Ü., "The conflict issue in international business and the global leadership." *Procedia- Social and Behavioral Science*, 41(2012): 100-107, p.105.
513 Zorlu & Hacıoğlu, *Conflict*, 105.
514 Zhang, M. Y., & Dodgson, M., "A roasted duck can still fly away: A case study of technology, nationality, culture and the rapid and early internationalization of the firm." *Journal of World Business*, 42(2007): 336–349. doi:10.1016/j.jwb.2007.04.005, p.336.
515 Zhang & Dodgson, *Internationalization*, 345.
516 Zhang & Dodgson, *Internationalization*, 346.
517 Zhang & Dodgson, *Internationalization*, 345.
518 Zhang & Dodgson, *Internationalization*, 347.

51

Leaders Focused on Personal Growth

In ensuring there is alignment in any environment, it has to start at the top with leaders. They must first embark on an introspective self-examination to determine an accurate perspective of their interest, concerns and levels of cultural literacy.[519] This requires an understanding of the facts about the cultures of various countries, their business procedures, and local information about customs and practices.[520] Another approach is to experience and learn these personally to help their companies interact sensitively with their international business contacts.[521] Leaders must also be exposed to the nuances of different cultures and languages to help them create alternative approaches that focus on goals, communicating clearly and exposing intentions.[522]

---

519 Cohen, S. L., "Effective global leadership requires a global mindset." *Industrial and Commercial Training*, 42(2010): p.3-10, p.8.
520 Cohen, *Global*, 8.
521 Cohen, *Global*, 8.
522 Cohen, *Global*, 8.

Examining the Motivation of Leaders

This is often cited as the main cause of failure of a company's expatriate staff to a new country.[523] To prevent this from occurring, leaders must possess sufficient motivation to help foreign hires apply their knowledge and skills effectively in their overseas postings.[524] The Intercultural Communication Motivation Scale (ICMS) is one of the major criteria for evaluating intercultural communication competence.[525] Expatriates who are motivated to establish intercultural relationships with staff and business contacts of their host countries tend to be more productive because they are able to adapt more quickly to the prevailing culture.[526] The ICMS consists of three elements: trust, anxiety and self-efficacy.[527]

Anxiety and trust issues can affect negatively an expatriate's perception of other cultures and hinder their ability to communicate effectively in the country they have been posted to work.[528] An effective expatriate staff is one who has high levels of trust and self-efficacy to initiate contact with the citizens of their host country to achieve their company's goals.[529] Implementing the ICMS can help recruiters assess a candidate' ability to communicate in an intercultural setting.[530] Recruiters and leaders can also use ICMS to evaluate if they are also able to communicate

---

523 Kraus, *Business*, 104
524 Atkins et al., *Intercultural*, 718.
525 Atkins et al., *Intercultural*, 718.
526 Atkins et al., *Intercultural*, 719.
527 Atkins et al., *Intercultural*, 720.
528 Atkins et al., *Intercultural*, 720.
529 Atkins et al., *Intercultural*, 720.
530 Atkins et al., *Intercultural*, 736.

effectively with people of another culture or as a predictive selection tool for new hires.[531] Appropriate training can then be designed to address deficiencies based on the ICMS results.

Transformational Leadership

Expatriates are sent overseas to transfer knowledge and they exercise control over affiliates in countries where local managerial talent is not readily available.[532] Transformational leadership styles influence innovation through providing support for creativity and tolerance of differences.[533] Leaders often provide positive feedback and acknowledgement to celebrate followers' contributions, which in turn enhances an individual's identification with the team and improves performance.[534]

Global Mind-set

The acquisition of a global mind-set will propel effective leadership in the international arena.[535] A global mentality is the ability to influence individuals, groups, organizations, and systems that have various intellectual, social, and psychological knowledge or intelligence.[536] It is no longer sufficient to simply think globally and act locally. It is now necessary to act both at the same time.[537] Leaders must be

---

531 Atkins et al., *Intercultural*, 736.
532 Elenkov & Manev, *Expatriate*, 357.
533 Elenkov & Manev, *Expatriate*, 359.
534 Elenkov & Manev, *Expatriate*, 360.
535 Cohen, *Global*, 9.
536 Cohen, *Global*, 5.
537 Cohen, *Global*, 5.

able to deepen their understanding of diverse cultures and contexts.[538] They must keep an openness and awareness to this diversity and possess the ability to incorporate them into the company.[539]

---

538 Cohen, *Global*, 6.
539 Cohen, *Global*, 6.

Qualities of a Global Leader

To lead an international company, a person must be able to think on a global scale, appreciate cultural diversity, build partnerships and alliances as well as share leadership responsibilities.[540] This new breed of leaders are also encouraged to have a deep sense of self-awareness, recognize their strengths and weaknesses, and have self-mastery.[541] They must also be conscious of the world, its cultures, nations and businesses.[542] Pre-requisites include a strong character, exhibited by a good set of habits that are others can emulate. These include honesty, trustworthiness, integrity and authenticity where their feelings, values and purpose are aligned with their actions.[543]

---

540 Cohen, *Global*, 6.

541 Howard, A., "A new global ethic." *Journal of Management Development,* 29(2010)5: 506 – 517, p.514.

542 Howard, *Global*, 515.

543 Howard, *Global*, 515.

Managing Global Teams

It is critical for a company that operates on a global scale to think beyond the national borders of its base for the good of the whole in terms of team development.[544] The leader must be able to lend assistance to all team members station in all parts of the world to manage change with confidence in the future in spite of disruptions and challenges that comes with it.[545] Such a leader must build teams that have mutually supportive interactive relationships.[546]

A win-win strategy

Team members must recognize the power of appreciating others and reinforce ownership of their value framework.[547] Inclusive behavior focuses on the ability to make management decisions and perform operations with a concern for the team, organization, industry and society.[548] Thus, in order for an organization to win, others must also win.[549]

Many global managers still reply primarily on logical, linear, black and white thinking.[550] Leadership teams must be able to sift through information and identify supportive and optimistic options that will enhance goal-achievement.[551] They need the ability to think logically while being more

---

544 Gabrielsson, Seristö, & Darling, "*Global*", 310.
545 Gabrielsson, Seristö, & Darling, "*Global*", 319.
546 Gabrielsson, Seristö, & Darling, "*Global*", 320.
547 Gabrielsson, Seristö, & Darling, "*Global*", 321.
548 Gabrielson, Seristö, & Darling, "*Global*", 318.
549 Gabrielsson, Seristö, & Darling, "*Global*", 318.
550 Gabrielsson, Seristö, & Darling, "*Global*", 313.
551 Gabrielsson, Seristö, & Darling, "*Global*", 314.

creative and innovative.[552] Positive emotions such as caring, hope and appreciation increase coherence, thereby energizing the organization.[553] Negative emotions such as frustration, conflict and stress decrease coherence and create exhaustion.[554]

---

552 Gabrielsson, Seristö, & Darling, "*Global*", 314.
553 Gabrielsson, Seristö, & Darling, "*Global*", 314.
554 Gabrielsson, Seristö, & Darling, "*Global*", 314.

Think Global, Act Local

Successful leaders are aware of their intentions, purpose driven and connected to their mission.[555] They must share this with their team members to help them remain consciously centered so that they are able to focus on issues of major importance and align their perceptions with the purpose.[556]

Focus on Applying Localized Solutions to Globalization

An organization needs to set a strategic global agenda of its strategic intent and interest which must be communicated to all employees.[557] Its vision and values must be globally consistency but its respective offices overseas must determine workplace practices and policy guidelines for the day-to-day running of their local operations.[558]

---

555 Gabrielsson, Seristö, & Darling, *"Global"*, 316.
556 Gabrielsson, Seristö, & Darling, *"Global"*, 316.
557 Cohen, *Global*, 9.
558 Cohen, *Global*, 9.

More recently, expansion of technology firms in emerging markets have been experiencing challenges on an organizational level that stretched from areas of human resource development, research and development (R&D), and marketing to managing cultural conflict management. Global businesses operate in substantially varying cultural, political and legal environments.[559] In China, multinational enterprises (MNE) such as Lenovo failed to expand globally because they lacked the capabilities to diffuse and leverage their managerial skills across international markets.[560] The Chinese often demand centralized and tangible control and eschews empowerment and ambiguity which ultimately makes managing more challenging.[561] Their organizational design provides for limited capacity to translate learning into competency because they are unable to spot and apply relevant knowledge that must be tailored to the needs of each national market.[562] These Chinese MNEs have had a problem adapting to cultures beyond their own home environment.[563]

Focusing on Global R&D Centers

On the other front, Huawei, China's largest tele-communications equipment manufacturer succeeded in internationalizing their operations by creating value-added

---

559 Gabrielsson, Seristö, & Darling, *"Global"*, 309.
560 Shenkar, O., "Becoming multinational : challenges for Chinese firms." *Journal of Chinese Economic and Foreign Trade Studies*, 2(2009):149-162. doi:10.1108/17544400910994733, p.158.
561 Shenkar, *Multinational*, 158.
562 Shenkar, *Multinational*, 158.
563 Shenkar, *Multinational*, 160.

technology products.[564] In establishing R&D centers globally, their structure was able to be international in nature but cross-cultural in composition.[565] The company focused on developing common build blocks (CBB) to give customers the confidence they adhere to an industry standard.[566] They could then customize products and services at reduced costs.[567] This location strategy allowed Huawei to keep their sites close to where strategic decisions are made and to ensure its voice is heard, as far as technical and market developments are concerned.[568]

Glocal Marketing

The idea to "think global, act local" is what is called the "Glocal strategy".[569] Global marketing that works in one country may not work in another.[570] To be successful across the world, companies must have a sound understanding of consumers' needs, wants, and requirements in each market.[571] A glocal marketing strategy can be defined as:

---

564 Low, B., "Huawei Technologies Corporation: from local dominance to global challenge?" *Journal of Business & Industrial Marketing*, 22(2007): 138-144, p.138.

565 Manardo, J., "Globalization at Internet Speed." *Strategy & Leadership*, 28(2000): 22-27, p.23.

566 Low, *Global*, 138.

567 Low, *Global*, 141.

568 Low, *Global*, 142.

569 Dumitrescu, L. & Vimerean, S., "The glocal strategy of global brands" *Studies in Business and Economics*. (2013) Sibiu, Romania

570 Svensson, G., "Beyond global marketing and the globalization of marketing activities." *Management Decision*, 40(2002): 574-583, p.580.

571 Svensson, *Globalization*, 580.

a compromise between the dogmatic, stereotype, and extreme marketing strategies between, on the one hand, adaptation, tailoring, difference, concentration, independence, flexibility, and separation of the focal firm's marketing activities, and on the other, standardization, homogenization, similarity, diffusion, dependence, synchronization, and integration of the focal firm's marketing activities.[572]

Glocal marketing recognizes the importance of local issues in its activities.[573] This concept is at best used at the strategic level.[574] It addresses the importance of harmony among a focal firm's marketing activities on operative, tactical and strategic levels.[575]

Training Framework

A program to get staff to be competent in the various cultures their company engages with, can help build understanding so that communication barriers are addressed and bridged.[576] The training framework can take the form of seminars, discussion groups or a library and information storage system.[577] It can cover the following areas:

- Recognizing and overcoming intercultural and intra-cultural boundaries. The former includes areas such as gender, political, class, education and religious

---

572 Svensson, *Globalization*, 580.

573 Svensson, *Globalization*, 579.

574 Svensson, *Globalization*, 581.

575 Svensson, *Globalization*, 581.

576 Qayyum, M. A., "Designing an intercultural training framework for information professionals." *Reference & User Services Quarterly*, 51 (2012): 227.

577 Qayyum, *Intercultural*, 227.

affiliation. Intra-cultural boundaries are more visible dissimilarities such as skin color, language or religious and social values;[578]

- Extending cultural comfort zones by encouraging to pair staff with a colleague from a different cultural background;[579]
- Identifying an intercultural "diversity champion". This person acts as a role model and is willing to reach out and communicate with people from other cultures;[580]
- Increasing intercultural understanding through exchange programs;[581] and
- Improved intercultural communication with an introduction to a beginners' business language course taught through task-based models and technology.[582]

---

578 Qayyum, *Intercultural*, 228.
579 Qayyum, *Intercultural*, 228.
580 Qayyum, *Intercultural*, 228.
581 Qayyum, *Intercultural*, 229.
582 Yang, H., "A proposal for transcending barriers of intercultural communication in global business: an instructional innovation." *Global Business Languages*, 14(2009): 29-40.

Rectifying the Intercultural Disconnect

An organization should consider adopting selected behavioral-focused cross cultural communication strategies for leaders to help overcome potential disconnect with various groups of people.[583] Even active listening is effective in overcoming barriers. It can involve restating and paraphrasing what a speaker says to clarify what the person actually means to communicate.[584] For those who use conference calls regularly, this creates a friendly environment that encourages everyone to speak.[585]

Where there is heavy reliance on written email correspondence and phone calls, the aim is to keep communication lines open and transparent to make up for the lack of visual cues. Conflicts are more easily resolved if this approach is standard practice.[586] This includes responding with appropriate words

---

583 Zofi, *Cross-cultural*, 8.
584 Zofi, *Cross-cultural*, 8.
585 Zofi, *Cross-cultural*, 8.
586 Zofi, *Cross-cultural*, 8.

that will not inflame a situation. Other behavioral strategies could include delivering balanced feedback, building on another person's ideas and giving credit or positive reinforcement.[587]

Leaders must also recognize the danger of their own assumptions and prejudgments that may be clouded by previous personal experiences and subconscious bias.[588] A global leader must, therefore, not attribute overgeneralize characteristics of a culture to any person. They also must refrain from stereotyping, be flexible and open to discussing other options, and to always find a middle ground and common interest rather than standing on position.[589] Sharing information about the team members' backgrounds is useful in these instances.

Multi-Dimensional Cultural Influence

The perceived abilities of leaders vary with each culture.[590] In some, people tend to rely more on a recognition-based process to perceive effectiveness of leadership. In others, people are more likely to adopt an inference-based way to do this.[591] The recognition-based perception involves pre-existing knowledge about leadership in a particular context such as information of underlying traits and behaviors.[592] Inference, on the other

---

587 Zofi, *Cross-cultural*, 8.
588 Zofi, *Cross-cultural*, 8.
589 Zofi, *Cross-cultural*, 8
590 Yan, J., & Hunt, J.G., "A cross cultural perspective on perceived leadership effectiveness." *International Journal of Cross Cultural Management : CCM*, 5(2005): 49-66. Retrieved from http://0-search.proquest.com.library.regent.edu/docview/221204922?accountid=13479, p.60.
591 Yan & Hunt, *Cultural*, 60.
592 Yan & Hunt, *Cultural*, 52.

hand, emphasizes the functional aspects of leadership as opposed to specific traits. People assume that a function of a leader is to produce good performance outcomes, and people infer leadership from knowledge of successful group or organizational performance.[593]

Yan & Hunt (2005) proposes that there is a need to examine cultural influence from a combination of different dimensions on leadership perception rather than one because it gives a more realistic picture.[594] However, what the total effects of these have on perception make cross-cultural comparison more difficult.[595] Yan & Hunt (2005) says that in cultures exhibiting high collectivism and femininity, they tend to prefer a recognition-based method. Conversely, a culture high in individualism and masculinity may have a stronger inclination to adopt an inference-based model.

In addition, good leadership effectiveness in terms of follower perception is related to cultural influences. In a society where a recognition-based process prevails, they rely more on whether leadership characteristics fit the implicit prototypes in the minds of their followers. The better the fit, the more the perception of their effectiveness.[596] But in cultures where an inference prevails, where performance outcome is the most important standard, leaders must rely on good performance rather than just fitting into some selected and expected characteristics. The better the performance outcomes, the

---

593 Yan & Hunt, *Cultural*, 51.
594 Yan & Hunt, *Cultural*, 58.
595 Yan & Hunt, *Cultural*, 58.
596 Yan & Hunt, *Cultural*, 61.

more effective they are perceived to be.[597] Therefore, the combined cultural influence on people's leadership perception modes in many countries will be determined by the relative strength of these opposite forces.[598]

---

597 Yan & Hunt, *Cultural*, 61.
598 Yan & Hunt, *Cultural*, 62.

Culture in Start-ups:
Not So Fast

Technology firms from emerging countries that have gone global have experienced tremendous growth in recent times. The structure and design of such an organization make it conducive for them to take advantage of any competitive positioning in new foreign markets. The team dynamics serve to minimize conflicts during these periods of exponential growth. The combination of the bird's eye view from the organizational, leader and team management levels serve as a guide for technology firms from such countries that are seeking to expand their operations globally.

These start-ups, especially in the technology sector, are constantly trying to create their own identity and culture. Generally, they have a high propensity for failure because of their reliance on the cooperation of strangers, their low levels of credibility and legitimacy, and their inability to compete effectively for resources.[599] To reduce these liabilities, new organizations need to manage their internal affairs first.[600] Once they have set up their internal systems, they must next form a culture.[601] This also takes time as everyone has to be together long enough to solve shared problems and observe the effect of their solutions.[602] Santaro and Sarros (2008) describes this stage as the growth phase and building a culture is necessary to ensure sustained growth that is consistent with an organization's mission.

Culture is the result of a cultivation of learning and reproduction of particular types of knowledge.[603] These are then inculcated, transmitted and expressed through social experiences.[604] Given the profound importance of a start-up's founders in developing its culture, they must communicate the vision that is grounded in realistic expectations.[605] But there is always the danger of working on culture too early. If this happens and comes with a grand vision statement and an instant set of supporting cultural values, it may come at a cost to the leadership's credibility.[606] The organization's members could also use the cultural knowledge in opportunistic ways that hinder collective pursuit.[607] The vision, therefore, needs to be

---

599 Pullen, W., "The start-up problem: Managing for credibility and cohesion in a new government agency." *The International Journal of Public Sector Management*, 5(1992): 28-38.
600 Pullen, *Start-up*, 32.
601 Pullen, *Start-up*, 35.
602 Pullen, *Start-up*, 35.
603 Lyon, *Cultural*, 178.
604 Lyon, *Cultural*, 178.
605 Lyon, *Cultural*, 198.
606 Pullen, *Start-up*, 35.
607 Lyon, *Cultural*, 176.

more than inspirational. It has to be plausible and attainable.[608] A participatory approach will provide a level of accountability between employees and executives. An open dialogue that encourages members' interests to be incorporated into the start-up's priorities will lead to a more achievable vision.[609]

Collective Effort

For technology start-ups, in particular, formation of culture should aim to maximize the efficiency of its employees. This can be done with a flat structure to promote effective communication.[610] And, if a start-up were to succeed in an ever-changing business environment, a "management by culture" is ideal.[611] It must also be designed to allow employees to communicate on-line to discuss its culture openly. Not only can this result in the creation of honest opinions about the company in public but employees can feel they belong and are part of a community.[612] Often, it could also end up delivering bottom-up solutions.[613]

The objective is to build a culture of "oneness" through the constant creation of strategic tools and delivery of training solutions for the business.[614] Another attribute of good culture is one that empowers individuals who also accept risk-taking.[615] Strengthening the companies' workforce

---

608 Lyon, *Cultural*, 198.
609 Lyon, *Cultural*, 199.
610 Cho & McLean, *IT*, 135.
611 Cho & McLean, *IT*, 135.
612 Cho & McLean, *IT*, 135.
613 Cho & McLean, *IT*, 135.
614 Cho & McLean, *IT*, 135.
615 Cho & McLean, *IT*, 136.

signals to employees the company values their talent and favors retaining them.[616]

Formalizing Culture Can Lead to Reduced Creativity

This development of culture must be guarded as it often could lead to formalization as it strives for efficiency. The downside to this is that it can adversely affect innovation.[617] In cases of smaller firms that have tried to formalize in order to revitalize their workforces, creativity was stifled.[618] Innovative learning is a creative activity that involves experimenting, risk-taking, and variance-seeking.[619] Supervision and control over creativity through formalized practices will weaken an innovative culture.[620] The reason technology start-ups can grow so rapidly is the fact that they are generally flexible and lack structure.[621] However, this often produces staff who are ill disciplined and this leads to an inefficient workflow. A balance between flexibility and less structure, and formalization and more controlled processes must be struck to help the company grow continually.[622]

Human Resource Development (HRD) practices have integrated areas such as training and development of the company and staff careers to improve their effectiveness.[623] Small firms, however, tend to have less HRD expertise,

---

616 Cho & McLean, *IT*, 137.
617 Cho & McLean, *IT*, 136.
618 Cho & McLean, *IT*, 136.
619 Cho & McLean, *IT*, 136.
620 Cho & McLean, *IT*, 136.
621 Cho & McLean, *IT*, 136.
622 Cho & McLean, *IT*, 137.
623 Cho & McLean, *IT*, 126.

infrastructure, and general resources that their bigger counterparts frequently enjoy.[624] Start-up firms must choose HRD practices carefully to manage and develop talent because they will shape the firms' innovative culture which, in turn, can affect growth.[625]

---

624 Cho & McLean, *IT*, 127.
625 Cho & McLean, *IT*, 137.

A Final Word

Culture is the glue that binds the initiatives leaders undertake in the journey of change as their companies take on the world. The TriNodic Leadership Model at its core highlights, firstly, the importance of leaders who inspire employees, who, as participants of change, are aligned with one another. They work and operate as a single unit who ultimately make change efficient and effective. However, an inspirational leader also requires that all employees are able to manage and make sense of the information available to them. This will ultimately allow the leaders, employees and ultimately the company to make informed decisions in a timely manner. Thus, decisiveness in leadership forms the second part of the TriNodic Leadership Model.

Inspirational leaders must function effectively in guiding companies through this competitive environment in ASEAN. To accomplish this, they have to understand that working as a united body is only possible if they are able to inculcate a focus on the future in their companies. It is also important for leaders to appreciate that this future centeredness will assist them to be ahead of competitors. This can be achieved by integrating a structured process of ensuring that the company is one big learning machine. It will allow them to absorb information constantly and to process before making decisions that are critical to help the company remain competitive in today's fast-paced business environment.

Being future centered makes up the third part to this TriNodic Leadership Model. With the appropriate culture and focus based on this model, a company is able to navigate through tomorrow's possible challenges by starting those critical structural changes, beginning today.

> **Take Away Messages (Chapters 43-56)**
>
> - The culture of an organization will be the determining force that operates in any organizational change;
> - Leaders need to understand what defines the culture of an organization;
> - Leaders need to appreciate the importance of culture and how it operates in a multi-cultural setting in Asia.

www.ingramcontent.com/pod-product-compliance
Lightning Source LLC
Chambersburg PA
CBHW031124130726
47988CB00006B/2211